P9-DMD-595

Southern
Folk Ballads
Volume II

AMERICAN
FOLKLORE
SERIES

Southern
Folk Ballads
Volume II

Compiled and edited by
W. K. McNeil

This Volume Is A Part Of

The American Folklore Series

W.K. McNeil, General Editor

August House / Little Rock
PUBLISHERS

Copyright 1988 by W. K. McNeil
All rights reserved. This book, or parts thereof,
may not be reproduced in any form without permission.
Published 1988 by August House, Inc.,
P.O. Box 3223, Little Rock, Arkansas, 72203,
501-663-7300.

Printed in the United States of America
10 9 8 7 6 5 4 3 2 1

LIBRARY OF CONGRESS CATALOGING-IN-PUBLICATION DATA
     _   Southern folk ballads.

(The American folklore series)
Unacc. melodies.
Each melody is followed by words printed as text
and commentary.
"Biblio-discography": v. 1, p. 167; v. 2, p. 179
Includes indexes.
1. Folk music—Southern States. 2. Ballads, English—Southern States
I. McNeil, W. K. II. Series.
M1629.6.S7S68 1987 87-751904
ISBN 0-87483-038-9 (alk. paper : v. 1)
ISBN 0-87483-039-7 (pbk. : v. 1)
ISBN 0-87483-047-8 (alk. paper : v. 2)
ISBN 0-87483-046-X (pbk. : v. 2)

First Edition, 1988

Cover design by Communication Graphics
Cover photograph from Collections
of the Library of Congress
Production artwork by Ira L. Hocut
Typography by Arrow Connection, Pollock Pines, CA
Musical notation by Jan Barger
Design direction by Ted Parkhurst
Project direction by Liz Parkhurst

This book is printed on archival-quality paper which meets the
guidelines for performance and durability of the Committee on
Production Guidelines for Book Longevity of the Council on
Library Resources.

AUGUST HOUSE, INC.   PUBLISHERS   LITTLE ROCK

Although the musical notation contains numerous errors, it appears here as originally published.

For Noble Cowden and to the memory of Almeda Riddle,
Southern folk ballad singers par excellence

Guide to reading musical notation

(1) All ballads are transcribed exactly as performed at the time of collection, even though there may be some irregularities in time, rhythm and notation.

(2) Time signatures enclosed in parentheses indicate that there will be variations from the stated time within the ballad.

(3) A short bar under a note indicates that that note is to be played or sung with special emphasis.

(4) In most cases, the melody line for a single verse is listed, although in cases where the melody differs from one stanza to another, the melody is listed either for the entire ballad or for the first stanza and the variant stanza.

Contents

Acknowledgments

Anyone with experience in book publishing knows that an author or editor is greatly relieved when his manuscript is completed. The editor of the present work is no exception to this general rule. Yet my delight at having finished this volume is no greater than my desire to acknowledge the help of those individuals without whom this book could not have been produced. They include Barry Jean Ancelet, Drew Beisswenger, Richard Blaustein, George W. Boswell, Dan Brackin, Thomas G. Burton, Kay L. Cothran, Frank de Caro, Dianne Dugaw, Burt Feintuch, Bill Ferris, George Foss, Bobby Fulcher, Ellen Garrison, Byrd Gibbens, Robert Halli, Don Hatley, Julie Henigan, Charles W. Joyner, Joyce Lamont, Bill Lightfoot, Ormond Loomis, Kip Lornell, Brenda McCallum, Bob McCarl, Tom McGowan, Roddy Moore, Dan Patterson, Dee Patterson, George Reinecke, Peter Roller, Sharon Sarthou, Mercedes Steely, John O. West, and Charles K. Wolfe. They were all gracious with their time and knowledge and much of what is worthwhile here is a result of their altruism. None of these people should be held accountable for any interpretations or errors found here; for those I claim sole responsibility.

W. K. McNeil

THE OZARK FOLK CENTER
MOUNTAIN VIEW, ARKANSAS

Introduction

This collection of ballads was mostly recorded since 1955 in the southern United States. Some are widely popular while others are known only in a relatively small area. A few originated in the South but most did not; instead they had their beginnings in various places ranging from the Old World to the commercial popular music industry of nineteenth- and twentieth-century America. They range in age from the early fifteenth century to the late 1920s. These certainly aren't the only ballads known in the South or necessarily even the most popular examples, although several of them would be found in any such listing. All of the ballads presented here are known in the South and, to that extent, they are representative Southern ballads although they are, in most cases, not unique to the region. Each song given here has been maintained by oral tradition and is thus an example of a folk ballad.

Several of these songs are taken from my own fieldwork, but most come from other collections and archives. I cannot claim that the informants whose contributions fill these pages were chosen by any design on my part. They just happened to have appropriate material that could be made immediately available to me. The method may seem somewhat haphazard but, because songs were sought from persons currently or recently doing ballad collecting in each state, the present selection does indicate to a considerable extent those areas where contemporary folksong fieldwork in the South has been concentrated. Evidently, my compilation is to a large degree dependent on the willingness of other collectors to share items with me and, although those people are credited in the acknowledgments, their unselfishness deserves mention here as well.

Obviously, many other volumes of Southern folk ballads could be compiled for not only can these materials be found in most communities in the South but folklorists, both amateur and professional, have spent many decades collecting ballads. Indeed, ballads may be the most frequently studied aspect of Southern folklore. This book, then, should be seen as an introductory rather than definitive work. In one respect, however, it is unique, namely in its attention to the entire South. Most ballad collections deal with one state or the entire nation or with a relatively small specific region like the Ozarks. There have even been collectors who did fieldwork in the entire South and there have been volumes dealing with ballads and folksongs of the western United States and New England, but, to my knowledge, no published collections dealing with the entire South. There is a book titled *Folksongs of the South* but it deals solely with West Virginia songs.

A number of terms used in this volume may be unfamiliar or confusing to many readers. First is the word *folklore,* which in popular usage is generally reserved for anything that is quaint or odd. That is not the exact meaning of the word, however, and not the one used in this book. Here, folklore refers to material that is passed on orally and, usually, informally; is traditional; undergoes change over space and time, creating variants and versions; is usually anonymous in the sense that most bearers of folklore are not concerned with the original creator; and finally, folklore is usually formulaic.[1]

Another definition essential for present purposes is *the South.* That is easily answered, for it refers to the states of Alabama, Arkansas, Florida, Georgia, Kentucky, Louisiana, Mississippi, North Carolina, South Carolina, Tennessee, Texas, and Virginia. In other words, the South is interpreted here as most of the states represented in the Confederacy during the Civil War. Admittedly, the Confederacy was a political rather than a cultural entity but these states do have a certain cultural and social unity although they definitely are not homogeneous. Moreover, these are the states often referred to when one speaks of "the South." Thus, logic is on the side of this particular drawing of the boundaries.[2]

A final term that must be defined is *ballad,* and to do so necessitates brief discussion of another word, *folksong.* Folklorists use the term *folksong* in two ways: as a generic word applied to all songs passed on by folksingers and as a means of distinguishing between lyric and narrative songs. *Ballad* is the term applied to folksongs that tell a story while folksong is reserved for those numbers that do not contain a narrative. But how much narrative does a song need to become a ballad? A song such as "I Can't Stay Here By Myself" which is made up entirely of "floating verses" (that is, verses found in numerous songs and seemingly fitting all equally well) would probably not be mistaken for a ballad even by novice folksong specialists. As the following lyrics make evident, it simply doesn't tell a connected narrative; it does suggest some story but never goes beyond the hint.

> Oh, I wish I was a little bird,
> I'd fly through the top of a tree,
> I'd fly and sing a sad little song,
> I can't stay here by myself.
>
> I can't stay here by myself,
> I can't stay here by myself.
> I'd fly and sing a sad little song,
> I can't stay here by myself.
>
> Once I had plenty money,
> My friends all around me would stand.
> Now my pockets are empty
> And I have not a friend in the land.

Farewell, farewell corn whiskey,
Farewell peach brandy too.
You've robbed my pockets of silver
And I have no use for you.

Oh, I wish I was a little fish,
I'd swim to the bottom of the sea.
I'd swim and sing a sad little song,
I can't stay here by myself.[3]

Likewise, it seems doubtful that any specialist would classify the number known variously as "The Creole Girl" or "The Lake of Pontchartrain" as anything other than a ballad:

It was on one Friday morning
I bid New Orleans adieu.
I made my way to Jackson
Where I was supposed to go.
Mid swamps and alligators
I made my weary way.
It was there I met that Creole girl
On the lake of Pontchartrain.

I said unto that Creole girl,
"My money to me is no good.
If it wasn't for the alligators
I'd sleep out in the woods."
"Oh, welcome, welcome stranger
Although our home is plain
We'll never turn a stranger down
On the lake of Pontchartrain."

She took me to her Mother's house
She treated me quite well.
Her hair in golden ringlets
Hung down [sic] her shoulders fell.
I tried to win her beauty
But I found it all in vain
To win the beauty of the Creole girl
On the lake of Pontchartrain.

I asked her if she'd marry me.
She said it could not be.
That you have a lover
And he was far off at sea.
"Oh, yes, you have a lover
And true you shall remain
Until he returns to you again
On the lake of Pontchartrain."

11

I said unto that Creole girl,
"Your face I shall see no more
I'll never forget the kindness
Or the cottage by the shore.
When· the moving sun shall circle
And sparkling drinks I'll drink.
I'll drink success to that Creole girl
On the lake of Pontchartrain."[4]

There are, however, many other songs that are not so obviously in one camp or the other. For example, consider the following songs (respectively, "Miss, I Have a Very Fine Horse," "My Father Was a Spanish Merchant," and "Waggoner's Lad"):

"Miss, I have a very fine horse
That stands in yonder stall,
That you may have at your command
If you will be my bride, bride, bride,
If you will be my bride."

"Sir, I see your very fine horse
That stands in yonder stall,
But he knows his master will get drunk
And's afraid that he will learn, learn, learn,
And's afraid that he will learn."

"Miss, I have a very fine house
That's been newly rectified,
That you may have at your command
If you will be my bride, bride, bride,
If you will be my bride."

"Sir, I see your very fine house
And also very fine yard
But who's to stay with me at night
When you are gambling and playing cards, cards,
Gambling and playing cards?"

"Miss, I never do that way
I never thought it right
But if you'll consent to marry me
I'll not stay out one night, night, night,
I'll not stay out one night."

"Sir, I know what that is for
It's just to take me in
And when you find the promise is true
You'll gamble and drink again, 'gain, 'gain,
You'll gamble and drink again!"

"Miss, I find you a very hard case
Perhaps too hard to please,
And some cold night when you are alone
I hope to my soul you'll freeze, freeze, freeze,
I hope to my soul you'll freeze."[5]

My father was a Spanish merchant
And before he went to sea,
He told me to be sure and answer,
"No," to all you said to me.
"No, sir! No, sir! No, sir! No!"

"If when walking in the garden
Plucking flowers all wet with dew
Tell me, would you be offended
If I walk and talk with you?"
"No, sir! No, sir! No, sir! No!"

"If I told you that I loved you
And would ask you to be mine
Tell me now, my pretty maiden,
Would you then my heart decline?"
"No, sir! No, sir! No, sir! No!"[6]

I am a poor girl, my fortune is sad
I've always been courted by a wagonner's lad,
He courted me gaily, by night and by day
And now he is loaded and going away.

Your horses are hungry, go feed them some hay.
Come sit down here by me as long as you stay.
My horses ain't hungry, they won't eat your hay,
So fare you well, darling, I'll be on my way.

Your wagon needs greasing, your whip needs to mend.
Come sit down here by me as long as you can.
My wagon is greasy, my whip's in my hand,
So fare you well darling, I'll no longer stand.[7]

Most folksong specialists would probably not classify either of the first two tunes here as a ballad but the third one is often so categorized. Yet even the most superficial observer would likely say that the first song contains more of a story than the last one does. That being the case, why would it not be called a ballad? The answer is that most folksong specialists have followed the lead of the eighteenth-century poet William Shenstone who referred to ballads as those songs in which action predominates over sentiment.[8] In actual practice, though, classification often proves to be arbitrary. Thus, Celestin P. Cambiaire categorized a version of "Waggoner's Lad" as a ballad while the editors of the *Frank C. Brown Collection of North Carolina Folklore* present it as a folksong.[9]

In the South, as elsewhere in the United States, three types of ballads are known: Child ballads, broadside ballads, and native American ballads. Child ballads are not so called because they are for or about children but because they are among the 305 ballads included by Francis James Child (1825–1896) in his multivolume work, *The English and Scottish Popular Ballads* (1882–1898). Child wrote in 1882 that he had gathered "every valuable copy of every known ballad,"[10] a statement that can now be recognized as too optimistic. In his defense it can be said that, given his specific definitions, few other examples of ballads have been discovered in the nearly ninety years since his tenth, and last, volume appeared. This lack of success, however, may be in part because for much of this time no one was looking for new ballads of the Child type. Until very recently folksong collectors prized the Child ballads above all others and sought out mainly variants and versions of them and, in many instances, ignored everything else. This antiquarian attitude was pronounced as recently as 1956 when an Appalachian folklore collector proclaimed that "The genuine *ballad* is only one type of folksong. Your 'ballad' is not a true *folk* ballad unless it is closely kin to one of the 305— no more, no less!—in Professor Child's great collection."[11]

Broadsides are a second category of traditional balladry. These are songs originally printed on one side of a sheet of paper and sold for a small fee. Many of these ballads found in Anglo–American tradition are classified in G. Malcolm Laws's *American Balladry from British Broadsides* (1957). Generally speaking, the broadsides are of more recent vintage than the Child ballads. The latter date from roughly 1500–1750 while broadsides mostly date from 1650–1900, although there are exceptions on both sides of the line. The lyrics of Child ballads and broadsides are frequently compared to tabloids for, like them, both kinds of ballads often deal with sensational subjects—robberies, murders, and the like being among their most common themes. But, examples are better than discussions so, for purposes of illustration, two ballad texts are given below, the first a Child ballad and the second a broadside. In the first of these, "Earl Brand" (Child 7), a girl is carried off by her lover. Her father and seven brothers pursue them. The ballad text explains the rest of the story:

> "Rise ye up, rise up my seven sons bold,
> Put on your armour bright,
> That it may not be said that a daughter of mine,
> Can stay with Lord Thomas overnight."

"Lady Margaret, my love, be brave," cried he,
"Hold this rein in your white hand,
That I may fight your seven brothers bold,
As in yonders green meadow they stand."

Lady Margaret did watch the battle so grim,
She never shed one tear,
Until she saw her seven brothers fall,
And the father she loved so dear.

"Lady Margaret, my love, will you go, will you go?
Or will you here abide?"
"Oh I must go, Lord Thomas, you know,
You have left me now without a guide."

He placed Lady Margaret on the milk white steed,
Himself upon the bay,
Drew his buckler down by his side,
And then rode bleeding away.

Lord Thomas died of his bloody, bloody wounds,
Lady Margaret died of grief,
Lady Thomas died from the loss of her son,
The eleventh one that must be.

They buried Lord Thomas on the church's right side,
Lady Margaret they laid upon the left,
They would not be parted before they died,
And they were united in death.

Out of one grave grew a climbing rose,
Out of the other grew a briar,
They grew till they met at the top of the church,
And they did grow no higher. [12]

The second ballad, "The Boston Burglar," was published in 1888, with Michael J. Fitzpatrick credited as author, but it is thought to be of British broadside origin. Certainly it predates 1888 and is similar to various ballads about Botany Bay (a British penal colony in Australia that was especially feared) that were probably its prototype. At some point in time the city of Boston was substituted for London, perhaps as a means of Americanizing it. The present version has a further localization by bringing in the name of Little Rock, Arkansas, probably more meaningful to the singer, who lived 135 miles from the Arkansas town, than the city of Boston which is over 1000 miles away.

I was born in Boston City, boys,
A city you all know well.
Raised up by honest parents,
The truth to you I'll tell.
Raised up by honest parents,
Raised up most tenderly.
Till I became a sporting young man
At the age of twenty-three.

My character was taken
And I was sent to jail.
Oh, the boys they found it all in vain
To get me out on bail.
The jury found me guilty,
The clerk he wrote it down.
Oh, the judge he passed a sentence, said he,
"You are bound for that Little Rock town."

They put me aboard this east-bound train
One cold December day.
And every station I'd pass through
I could hear those people say,
"There goes that Boston Burglar,
With iron strong chains he's bound down,
For some bad crime or other,
To be sent to that Little Rock town."

There lives a girl in Louisville,
A girl that I love well.
If ever I gain my liberty,
Along with her I'll dwell.
If ever I gain my liberty,
Bad company I will shun.
Likewise nightwalk and gambling,
And also drinking rum.

You who have your liberty;
Please keep it while you can.
And don't run around with boys at night
And break the laws of man.
For if you do you surely will
Find yourself like me,
Just serving out twenty-three long years
In the state penitentiary.[13]

Of course, not all Child ballads or broadsides deal with such serious matters. One of the more popular Child ballads in the South is "Our Goodman" (Child 274). This and several other of the 305 Child pieces are comic numbers. The same can be said for the broadsides, an example of which is the following number of British origin that is known by various titles but called by the informant "Rich Old Lady."

I knew a rich old lady,
In London she did dwell.
She loved her husband dearly,
But other men twice as well.
Sing penny a wink she randolph,
Sing penny a wink she roan.

She went to the doctor
In hopes that she might find
Some kind of medicine
To make her husband blind.
Sing penny a wink she randolph,
Sing penny a wink she roan.

She gave him two marrow bones
And told him to suck them all.
And then he said, "My dear little wife
I cannot see you at all."
Sing penny a wink she randolph,
Sing penny a wink she roan.

"I think I'm going to drown myself,
If I only knew the way."
"Here, let me take you by the hand,
As you might go astray."
Sing penny a wink she randolph,
Sing penny a wink she roan.

Well, she walked on the banks,
And she walked on the shore.
And he said, "My dear little wife
You'll have to push me o'er."
Sing penny a wink she randolph,
Sing penny a wink she roan.

She took a few steps backwards
And run to push him in.
He just stepped to one side
And let her tumble in.
Sing penny a wink she randolph,
Sing penny a wink she roan.

Now, she began to holler,
And she began to squall.
But he said, "My dear little wife
I cannot see you at all."
Sing penny a wink she randolph,
Sing penny a wink she roan.

> *The old man being good-natured,*
> *And afeared that she might swim,*
> *He run and cut a big long pole*
> *And pushed her further in.*
> *Sing penny a wink she randolph,*
> *Sing penny a wink she roan.*
>
> *Now my little song is over*
> *And I won't sing it no more.*
> *But wasn't she a blamed old fool*
> *For not swimming to the shore.*[14]

One feature of many Child ballads found in the Old World that differs from the same songs found in the South, or elsewhere in the United States, is the elimination of magic and supernatural elements. For example, many Old World versions of "The Two Sisters" contain the supernatural motif of the singing instrument which is missing in most Southern versions. The first version of this ballad given in this collection is thus typical of Southern treatments. However, the "Wind and Rain" version also given here indicates that the supernatural elements of the ballad are not missing altogether in Southern renditions, although even here the singing instrument motif is greatly changed. There is nothing particularly magical about the instrument except that only one tune can be played on it. In older versions of "James Harris" (The Daemon Lover) (Child 243), which is commonly known in the South as "The House Carpenter" or "The House Carpenter's Wife," a revenant or the Devil comes to carry off a woman. As usually found in the South, the ballad simply describes a love triangle.

Along with the general tendency to eliminate supernatural and magic elements is a tendency to dispense with, or at least to diminish the importance of, sex, incest, and kin-murder. For example, older versions of "The Two Brothers" (Child 49) tell of jealousy arising because of an incestuous relationship with their sister. Southern versions, such as "Two Little Boys Were Going to School," typically have the brothers fight over a more trivial matter—the failure to play ball:

> *Two little boys were going to school,*
> *And fine little boys were they.*
> *I truly wish myself with them,*
> *My playmates for to be.*
> *I truly wish myself with them,*
> *My playmates for to be.*

> *Oh, Johnny can you toss the ball?*
> *Or can you fling a stone?*
> *I am too little, I am too young,*
> *Dear brother leave me alone.*
> *I am too little, I am too young,*
> *Dear brother leave me alone.*
>
> *Then Willie pulled out his pocket knife,*
> *He had it keen and sharp,*
> *Between the long ribs and the short*
> *He pierced poor John to the heart,*
> *Between the long ribs and the short*
> *He pierced poor John to the heart.*[15]

Obviously there are exceptions to these generalizations for there are Child ballads still traditional in the South that include supernatural elements, as the section of my second volume devoted to such songs clearly indicates. Usually the supernatural motifs are assumed without actually being stated.

Native American ballads, the third category of traditional ballads, are more numerous than either Child ballads or British broadsides and mostly date from 1850 to the present. There are exceptions, though, for "The Rattlesnake Song" is thought to be considerably older. Like broadsides, the native American ballads deal largely with scandals and tragedies, although themes of American history and developments are also found. Then, too, there are many like "The Big Crap Game" which are merely humorous:

> *Well, I went out to a big crap game,*
> *It was against my will.*
> *Bet all my money*
> *Except one greenback dollar bill.*
> *Was a hundred dollars on the table,*
> *And the feelings they were high.*
> *Just then a cop came through the door*
> *And I got mine.*
>
> *I got mine, boys,*
> *I got mine.*
> *I grabbed that hundred dollars,*
> *Through the window I did climb.*
> *For a while I was a-wearin' good clothes,*
> *Livin' on chicken and wine.*
> *Was a leader in society*
> *When I got mine.*

Well, I went into a big cafe,
I went in there to dine,
I only had fifteen cents,
But was full of good white wine.
I ate everything on the table,
I was feelin' mighty fine.
And I handed over that fifteen cents
And I got mine.

I got mine, boys,
I got mine.
They used me for a football;
At kicking they was fine.
They kicked me through the window,
I got there just in time.
A policeman took me to the judge
And I got mine.

Well, I went to get some chickens,
The night was very fine.
I found them roostin' very high
And for them I did climb.
A bulldog came prowlin' round,
He got there just in time.
He got me by the seat of the pants
And he got mine.

He got mine, boys,
He got mine.
The rascal took my britches,
He did it very fine.
I went home in a barrel,
I got there just in time.
I used some Dr. Brown's Salve
Where he got mine.[16]

Several native American ballads, such as "The Fatal Wedding," are not cited in G. Malcolm Laws's *Native American Balladry* (1950; revised 1964), the standard bibliographic guide to these songs, because they are known to originate in the popular music industry. For the same reason such songs have often been overlooked by ballad collectors whose interest generally runs to older ballads of unknown authorship. In so doing they have slighted an important aspect of American balladry and, in a sense, distorted the picture of traditional singing in the United States.

Traditional ballads—whether Child, broadsides, or native American—all have distinctive characteristics. All three types generally concentrate on a single episode. Typical is the following version of "The Dying Brakeman" which focuses on a tragedy in which the motorman of a mine train is unable to stop the cars in time to prevent them from running over his brakeman:

See that true and trembling brakeman,
As he falls between the cars!
Not a moment's warning has he;
From those freight cars he is hurled.

See those car wheels passing o'er him,
O'er his mangled body and head;
See his sister bending o'er him,
Crying, "Brother, are you dead?"

"Dying, sister, yes, I'm dying;
Going to join that other shore;
For our father and our mother
I shall never see no more.

"Sister, when you see our brother,
These few words I send to him;
Never, never venture braking;
If he does, his life will end."[17]

Narratives in ballads are advanced primarily by means of dialogue. Some ballads are told entirely in dialogue but most alternate stanzas of dialogue with stanzas of action, with a bit of description mingled in. Typical is the following localized version of "The Gypsy Laddie" (Child 200), which is called, "When Carnal First Came to Arkansas":

When Carnal first came to Arkansas,
He came from Missouri O.
He sung so sweet and melodious
That he charmed the heart of a lady O.

When the landlord came in at night,
Inquiring for his lady O,
The answer was, "She is not here;
She's run away with Carnal."

Go saddle to me my little bay mare;
The black is not so speedy O.
I'll ride all day, I'll ride all night,
Or I'll overtake my lady.

Won't you turn around? Won't you come back?
Won't you go with your husband O?
I'll lock you up in a room so high,
Where Carnal can't come nigh you.

I won't turn around, nor I won't go back;
I won't go with my husband O.
I wouldn't give a kiss from Carnal's lips
For all your land and your money.

They rode east and they rode west,
They spent most all her money O,
Likewise the gold pins off her breast,
The gold rings off of her finger.

I used to have a house and home
And seven little babes to enthrall me O.
Now I've come to the want of bread,
And Carnal's gone and left me. [18]

The narrative approach in Child ballads is impersonal with little or no intrusion of the narrator's point of view. Even where the singer may be sympathetic with the protagonist's plight, such view is not explicitly stated. The same, to a lesser extent, can be said for both broadsides and native American ballads. Like modern journalism, ballads focus on the climax of an action and its result, giving the happenings in as straightforward, objective a manner as possible. The description of the duel in the version of "Little Massie Grove" (Child 81) contained in Volume I of this work is a perfect example of the impersonality of the Child ballads as is this description of a murder in "Love Henry" (Child 68):

He went to the bed to little Marg'ret
And give her a farewell kiss.
And with a penknife in her right hand
She wounded him full death.
And with a penknife in her right hand
She wounded him full death. [19]

All of the preceding characteristics are typically found in Child ballads and are often present in broadsides and native American ballads as well. They can be considered primary characteristics while some other features found in many Child, and other types of, ballads are not essential. Many songs begin *in medias res*, that is, in the middle of the story. "The House Carpenter's Wife" (Child 243) which, in many versions, begins not with a detailed description of the scene but, rather, with the two principal figures greeting each other by saying "well met, well met" is a perfect example of this feature. The background is pieced together by the listener as the ballad progresses. Such a characteristic may reflect a loss during the process of transmission and reflects the tendency of ballads to retain only details that are absolutely essential.

Another characteristic often found in ballads is called leaping and lingering. This refers to the tendency to treat individual scenes in detail and then shift the narrative to another scene with little or no transition. Various kinds of repetition are also common; at least five different types occur regularly. These include plain repetition where words, phrases, or stanzas are simply repeated. There is also the climax of relatives in which

22

songs consist largely and sometimes entirely of references to various members of one's family. "Jimmy Loud" and "Hangman" (Child 95) in Volume I of this work are excellent examples of the climax of relatives. A third type of ballad repetition is incremental repetition in which the story is advanced by repeating nearly the same lines with minor changes that advance, or increment, the narrative. A perfect example of this type of repetition is the following version of "The Three Maids" (Child 11):

There was three maids a-playing ball, I lily-O
There was three maids a-playing ball, I lily-O
They some three lords for to court them all,
For the rose is sweet I know.

The foremost one was dressed in red, I lily-O
The foremost one was dressed in red,
And this is the one I make my wed,
For the rose is sweet I know.

The middle one was dressed in green, I lily-O
The middle one was dressed in green,
And this is the one I'll make my queen,
For the rose is sweet I know.

The foremost one was dressed in white, I lily-O
The foremost one was dressed in white,
Oh this is the one I'll make my wife,
For the rose is sweet I know.

Her brother John was standing by, I lily-O
Her brother John was standing by,
He wounded his sister with a knife
For the rose is sweet I know.

Ride on, ride on, to yonder's hill, I lily-O
Ride on, ride on, to yonder's hill,
Till I get down and bleed a while,
For the rose is sweet I know.

Ride on, ride on, to yonder's hill, I lily-O
Ride on, ride on, to yonder's hill,
Till I get down and make my will,
For the rose is sweet I know.

What do you will your sister Ann? I lily-O
What do you will your sister Ann?
My trunk of gold and silver pan,
For the rose is sweet I know.

What do you will your true love dear? I lily-O
What do you will your true love dear?
This snow white horse that I rode here,
For the rose is sweet I know.

What do you will your mother dear? I lily-O
What do you will your mother dear?
My snow white dress what I wore here,
For the rose is sweet I know.

Tell her to wash it nice and clean, I lily-O
Tell her to wash it nice and clean,
So my heart's blood can never be seen,
For the rose is sweet I know.[20]

Other types of ballad repetition include speech and action in which in one stanza a person is instructed to perform some action which he does in the next stanza. Finally, in some ballads a stanza is repeated, the repetition serving as a means of transition.

Many of these non-essential characteristics frequently occurring in Child ballads are often found in both broadsides and native American ballads. Broadsides, however, differ from Child ballads in that they frequently use the "Come all ye" opening stanza and are often narrated in the first person. Native American ballads are much more likely than the others to include a moral at the ending although older ballads have on several occasions been altered in Southern tradition to include comments of a moralizing nature. All three types of ballads generally have a short narrative, simple action, chronologically arranged scenes, a limited number of characters (usually two, rarely more than four), and hardly ever any action after the climax.

Having made these working definitions and outlined certain characteristics of ballads, it remains to note that ballads are not superorganic. That is, they do not exist by themselves but are, rather, kept alive by various singers. That may seem to be belaboring the obvious, yet at one time ballad collectors presented their texts as though they were maintained in some mysterious manner in which human beings played no part. Fortunately, that era is past, but even now most ballad collections have little more on the informant (the person the material was recorded from) than the name and date of collection. One of the shortcomings of the present volume is that in several cases I was unable to obtain anything more than the sketchiest data on informants. Whatever was available is given in the notes that follow each entry.

Granted that individual singers keep the ballads alive, the question arises: who are these ballad singers? What type of person maintains these traditions? The answer is, of course, that many different types of people are folk ballad singers. There is a certain degree of truth in the dogmatic claim set forth in 1951 by a prominent student of the ballad that folksingers are characterized by (1) living in a rural or isolated region which (2) "shuts [them] off from prolonged schooling and contact with industrialized urban civilization, so that (3) [their] cultural training is oral rather than visual."[21] He is correct because some traditional singers do meet all three of these requirements, but he is also wrong because many others do not. Indeed, if anything, the exceptions outweigh the rule. True, a singer like the late Almeda Riddle was from a rural background and did not have an extensive formal education. That does not mean that her whole cultural training was oral or that she had no knowledge of, or contact with, urban civilization. Anyone who ever met her knows that those characteristics simply didn't apply in her case.

For several of the informants Edwin Kirkland recorded in Tennessee during the 1930s and 1940s none of the three characteristics mentioned applies. His best sources of folk ballads were, in several instances, city residents who were highly educated, about whom it could not be said that their cultural training was entirely oral. For example, one of his best finds, a rare version of "Sir Patrick Spens" (Child 58), was collected in 1937 from Clara J. McCauley who had learned it from other members of her family. McCauley, the Supervisor of Public School Music in Knoxville, Tennessee, was an urban woman with an above average amount of formal education, hardly someone who could be described as a rustic illiterate out of contact with the modern world. Yet her ballad was fully traditional by the strictest definition of folklore. Kirkland turned up many other good urban folk ballad singers, people like Columbus Popejoy, a Knoxville bank teller who was also a superb raconteur. Kirkland even found great traditional ballad singers among faculty members of the University of Tennessee. He recognized that, at the time, such settings were not where most people sought "songs in the genuine folk tradition," adding that "I held this opinion when I first began to collect, but before very long I found that faculty members not only were interested in folksongs but also had learned some of them in the true folk manner."[22] In all, roughly one third of Kirkland's large collection of folk ballads came from such highly educated, urban, but traditional singers as the University of Tennessee faculty or Clara McCauley.

Despite the evidence to the contrary the popular conception of a traditional balladeer is that of a rustic, unschooled illiterate. As already mentioned it was once the view of most ballad scholars and, even today, has a few adherents in the academic world, admittedly mainly among those who don't do fieldwork. Yet, if the bulk of evidence refutes such a view why has it persisted? There are, of course, many possible explanations. One is that academics like to view things in black and white terms when, in actuality, most things are gray. There is, in other words, a tendency to offer the perfect example as the only example. There is no doubt about the folk nature of someone who lives removed from contact with everything but the "purest" folk cultures. It seems doubtful that any such society, or even person, ever existed in America. A second possible reason for the longevity of the rustic, unschooled illiterate concept of ballad singers is simply that it is romantic and somehow exotic to think of the folk as being creatures who are colorful and live in picturesque bucolic settings. The folk ballad singer has, in some cases, replaced the noble savage of past centuries. There is also the unfortunate fact that some collectors and authorities tend to view the folk as inferiors who are to be pitied and, in most cultural situations, avoided. It is worth noting here that ballad singers are also often stereotyped as being poor. To those holding this view the folk are always seen as someone different from themselves, charmingly quaint but also somehow disgusting people who must be consigned to some place other than that in which most people live. Finally, the rustic illiterate concept of folk ballad singers is often perpetuated because the tacit assumption is made that "folk," "popular," and "academic" culture are three distinct levels which never interact. Thus, one can function on only one level at a time and they exist in tiers with "folk" culture at the bottom and "academic" culture at the top. In reality all three levels are on the same tier and there is interaction between them all the time; thus it is possible to function in more than one area simultaneously. Contrary to the stereotype, folksingers are found everywhere, from the most rural to the most urban settings. They do not exist in a world that no one else inhabits but function, for better or worse, in the same world all of us live in. Briefly put, geographic area, financial status, educational background, political inclinations, or other similar factors have nothing to do with determining whether or not a person is a ballad singer. No matter where or how they live, ballad singers are intelligent people with good memories who have an interest in, and are willing to sing ballads.

There are many people blessed with intelligence and good memories who have an interest in ballads but simply aren't good ballad singers. They are what the Swedish folklorist Carl Wilhelm von Sydow labeled *passive bearers of tradition.* Unlike active tradition bearers "the passive bearers have indeed heard of what a certain tradition contains, and may perhaps when questioned, recollect part of it, but do nothing themselves to spread it or keep it alive."[23] It seems that Dorothy Oswald, a student at the University of Arkansas, from whom Irene Carlisle collected a version of "The Great Titanic," was such a passive traditional ballad singer. She gave Carlisle the words to the song, which she had from traditional sources, and even recalled the melody but did not sing it even though she was aware of the collector's interest in obtaining melodies for the songs she gathered. On the other hand, the late Fred High, one of Arkansas's best known traditional singers, was in every sense a person who helped "keep tradition alive and transmit it,"[24] even going so far as printing seventy-three of the ballads he knew in a small paperback book which was sold primarily in the area around his home near Berryville, Arkansas. High had a keen sense of the value of the ballads he knew and sang for his own community and was always willing to sing for collectors. As a result numerous recordings of his singing are available today in various folklore archives.

Passive bearers of ballads, as well as other types of folklore, do play a significant role. Von Sydow noted that passive carriers of a tradition give it resonance. That is, they reinforce and prolong a tradition by providing it with an audience. It is, of course, possible for a singer to sit and sing ballads to himself but it is not likely that the songs are going to remain in tradition long if the singer is his sole audience. Passive bearers also act, to some extent, as a check on tradition. If, for example, some change is made in a ballad the passive singer, being familiar with the song, can easily correct it, "and they do so, which is of great importance for the unchanging survival of the tradition."[25]

A not uncommon situation is for passive and active bearers to change their relationship to folk tradition. Passive bearers might become active if they hear a tradition long enough that they become conversant with it and take it actively in hand. On the other hand, active bearers may become passive for various reasons. For example, a child may know several children's folksongs but become passive concerning them once he has outgrown his childhood. As noted above, an active bearer may also become passive when there is no longer an audience for the traditions he knows. Usually, though, active and passive ballad singers remain so all their lives.

Granted that there are both active and passive ballad singers, where do they perform? What is the environment in which folk ballads are sung? The answer is simple: they are sung just about anywhere, although generally before an audience of at least one other person besides the singer. Unlike some other genres of folklore, such as the proverb or legend, ballads often are performed by a singer for his own enjoyment in situations where no one else is around. In most instances, though, there is some other audience involved, typically a small one. Usually the distance between the singer and the audience is not so great as that between a concert pianist and those attending his recital. There is also often much more interplay between the singer and audience than is commonly the case in formal concerts.

Almeda Riddle (1898–1986) related an amusing incident concerning the effect her singing had on one audience. It is quoted here in full not only because it shows the context of some ballad singing but also because it reveals much about the typical relationship between a folksinger and the audience. "I remember one time we were picking cotton— as a child I was in the cotton patch—I think I was seven years old at the time and I'd first heard this 'No Telephone in Heaven,' and I sang it over and over all day long. I couldn't think of anything else until finally a man offered me a quarter. Now, a quarter at that time—as a child twenty-five

27

cents meant as much as a dollar and a half would mean to a child now. Well, this man, he gave me twenty-five cents if I would please just not sing 'No Telephone in Heaven' again that day. And the next day I could sing it all I wanted to."[26]

Given that traditional ballad singers perform just about anywhere, the question remains: why do they sing ballads? Again, it is relatively easy to answer the query even though until approximately twenty-five years ago most collectors did not bother to ask their informants about such matters. Still, the clues that do exist suggest a myriad of reasons, almost as many as one can imagine. Among the most important are that a singer likes the story told in a ballad's lyrics, or likes the tune, or both. Some see it as a way of preserving their own past; others think of ballads as an important, and fun, portion of local history. For example, a ballad like "Lula Viers" in this volume may be to the traditional singer from Kentucky an accurate account of a local tragedy. Often a ballad is kept alive because it was associated with a beloved person close to the singer. Sometimes the ballad is perpetuated because of the lesson it teaches, sometimes because it is considered a classic. There are, of course, many other possibilities but these are sufficient to make the point that there is no single reason that explains why traditional singers perform ballads.

Almeda Riddle provided a good capsule summary of why she chose the songs she sings. Speaking of "classic" ballads she said: "A classic ballad is something you class highly, something in your idea. Maybe what someone else would call a classic I wouldn't. 'Lady Margaret,' a nice version of it, I think that's a classic. This 'Four Marys' I consider that one too—to me, maybe not to you. And a variant of this 'Hangman's Tree' that is very old—I found this back in about, I believe, in about the fifteenth century in an old Scottish book. And almost this version. Almost exactly like this is, and I'd been singing it then for forty years.

"But I don't think the age has everything to do with a classic. You might write a classic. Something that would be classical—would teach something, be worth preserving. It could be dirty and old and trash and not teach anything and be a thousand years old and still would be that when it started out. That's what the word 'classic' to me means. That teaches something that's worth remembering, that's worth passing on."[27]

One other consideration concerning ballad singers merits attention, namely the manner in which they perform. Any folksinger or, for that matter, anyone who is an active bearer of any kind of folklore, presents his material in a specific manner. Southern traditional singers perform in an impersonal or objective style. The singers maintain one tempo, one level of intensity, one timbre throughout a song. They remain, in a sense, detached from the lyrics and never resort to any intrusions that detract from the ballad. A routine stanza providing plot background is given equal attention with a stanza that contains the dramatic climax. No sudden diminuendo (lowering of volume) or crescendo (increasing volume), such as the art or popular singer employs to spotlight important points in a song, is used. For traditional ballad singers in the South, as elsewhere in America, the text is of major importance; all else is secondary. When, in "Barbara Allen," William calls her to his deathbed, the meeting would be treated by the art singer as a very significant part of the song, its importance emphasized by the use of such musical dynamics as diminuendos or crescendos or ritardandos (slowing down), whereas the folk singer treats these stanzas no differently than any other in the ballad.

All that remains is some explanation of the categories used in the present book. Basically they follow the categories outlined in the two books by G. Malcolm Laws, *American Balladry From British Broadsides* and *Native American Balladry,* the standard bibliographic guides to all American folk balladry but, as any observer can tell, do not follow them exclusively. The changes were necessitated by the material that I was able to accumulate from other sources in a relatively short time. I am fully aware that arranging the ballads by textual considerations tends to ignore the importance of ballad music, but in my defense I offer the argument that it is the method most often used by editors of ballad collections and therefore has tradition on its side. Moreover, I am fully aware that ballads are not superorganic, that they are kept alive in tradition by people. These categories are offered only as a convenient means of ordering the material at hand, not as an ironclad arrangement of texts. Indeed, some songs could just as easily be placed in another category than the one it is given in here, but that is also a problem with the Laws categories. Despite the admitted flaws of this method of presentation, I believe it does include the major themes of Southern folk balladry. One other note of caution: a low number of selections given here under a specific category does not necessarily indicate the degree of popularity of that theme in Southern folk balladry, but only shows that I was unable to obtain a larger supply of songs on that particular topic in time for inclusion.

The main reason for putting together a collection of ballads is to have people read, enjoy, and, if they wish, sing them. To facilitate singing I have included, wherever possible, a melody transcription, in a few cases taking a melody line from some other source than the person whose text is given here. In all those instances where no melody line is given there was none available to me either from collector, informant, or alternative source. Those texts with melodies provided from alternative sources are clearly indicated; in all other cases the melody is as sung by the informant who is identified. The accompanying headnotes provide historical information on each ballad.

One final comment: it is customary for editors of folksong and ballad collections to lament the passing of these items. Such volumes are often presented in a funerary spirit that would lead one to believe that the gems they contain were destined to disappear from earth forever. That is not the attitude of the present editor, who hopes this collection will demonstrate that folk balladry is not only alive in the South but is flourishing. True, it probably doesn't exist in the same way it did in eighteenth-century England, but then, folk balladry of that era was not exactly the same as that found in England two centuries earlier. Folk ballad singing has undergone change in the past and most likely will again, but it is a long way from being dead. In fact, the almost constant change, enabling Southern folk balladry to adapt to changing conditions, may be the one thing that has insured the survival of the tradition.

W. K. McNeil
THE OZARK FOLK CENTER

Notes

[1]For a more detailed discussion of these points, see my book *The Charm Is Broken: Readings in Arkansas and Missouri Folklore* (Little Rock: August House, Inc., 1984), pp. 11–13.

[2]On the matter of where "the South" is see John Shelton Reed, *The Enduring South: Subcultural Persistence in Mass Society* (Chapel Hill: The University of North Carolina Press, 1982) and the same author's *Southerners: The Social Psychology of Sectionalism* (Chapel Hill: The University of North Carolina Press, 1983). The states I have included in "the South" do not entirely agree with a table given in *The Enduring South,* p. 16, but Reed notes, p. 14, that persons involved in the survey were not asked to comment on whether Kentucky was a Southern state or not.

[3]Collected in 1979 by W.K. McNeil from Bob Blair, Pleasant Grove, Arkansas. Blair's version of the song can be heard on *Not Far From Here . . . : Traditional Tales and Songs Recorded in the Arkansas Ozarks.* Arkansas Traditions, no number.

[4]Collected in 1979 by W.K. McNeil from Rance Blankenship, Melbourne, Arkansas. Blankenship's version can be heard on *Not Far From Here.*

[5]Collected May 14, 1963 by Mrs. Robert J. Snyder from the singing of Mrs. Deans Crumpler and Susan Harriet Snyder, Columbia, South Carolina.

[6]*Ibid.*

[7]Text quoted from Roger D. Abrahams and George Foss, *Anglo–American Folksong Style* (Englewood Cliffs, New Jersey: Prentice–Hall, Inc., 1968), pp. 40–41.

[8]Shenstone is quoted in volume III of *The Frank C. Brown Collection of North Carolina Folklore* (Durham: Duke University Press, 1952), p. 3.

[9]See Brown, III, 275 and Celeste P. Cambiaire, *East Tennessee and Western Virginia Mountain Ballads* (London: The Mitre Press, 1935), p. 37.

[10]Francis J. Child, *The English and Scottish Popular Ballads,* I (New York: Dover Publications, Inc., 1965; reprint of a work originally issued in 1882), vii.

[11]Richard Chase, *American Folk Tales and Songs* (New York: The New American Library of World Literature, Inc., (1956), p. 229.

[12]Collected by George Foss in 1961 from Robert Shiflett, Brown's Cove, Virginia.

[13]Collected by W.K. McNeil, August, 1977 from Rance Blankenship, Melbourne, Arkansas. Blankenship can be heard singing the song on *Not Far From Here.*

[14]Collected in 1979 by W.K. McNeil from Kenneth Rorie, Batesville, Arkansas. Rorie can be heard singing the song on *Not Far From Here.*

[15]Collected by W.K. McNeil, April 25, 1979, from Mrs. Alice Best, Fox, Arkansas.

[16]Collected by W.K. McNeil in 1979 from Bob Blair, Pleasant Grove, Arkansas. Blair can be heard singing the song on *Not Far From Here.*

[17]Collected by Irene Jones Carlisle, June 29, 1951, from Lewis Bedingfield, Springdale, Arkansas.

[18]Collected by Theodore R. Garrison, July, 1942, from Mrs. Zona Baker, Zack, Arkansas.

[19]Collected by George Foss in 1958 from Marybird McAllister, Brown's Cove, Virginia.

[20]Collected by Herbert Halpert, Emory L. Hamilton, and an unidentified woman, March 24, 1939, from Polly Johnson, Wise, Virginia. Johnson can be heard singing the song on *Virginia Traditions: Ballads From British Tradition* BRI-002.

[21]Joseph W. Hendron, "The Scholar and the Ballad Singer," in MacEdward Leach and Tristram P. Coffin, *The Critics and the Ballad* (Carbondale and Edwardsville: Southern Illinois University Press, 1961), p. 7. Hendron's article originally appeared in *The CEA Critic.*

[22]Quoted in the booklet accompanying Tennessee Folklore Society album TFS-106 *The Kirkland Recordings,* p. 3.

[23]C.W. von Sydow, *Selected Papers of Folklore* (New York: Arno Press, 1977; reprint of a work originally published in 1948), pp. 12–13.

[24]See Carlisle's M.A. thesis *Fifty Ballads and Songs From Northwest Arkansas* submitted at the University of Arkansas in 1952, p. 84.

[25]von Sydow, p. 14.

[26]Roger D. Abrahams, *A Singer and Her Songs: Almeda Riddle's Book of Ballads* (Baton Rouge: Louisiana State University Press, 1970), pp. 108–109.

[27]*Ibid.,* pp. 109, 111.

Humorous Ballads

Billy Grimes

COLLECTED BY BYRON ARNOLD FROM MAY RANDLETTE BECK, MOBILE, ALABAMA, JULY 8, 1947. TRANSCRIPTION BY BYRON ARNOLD.

"Tomorrow morn I'm sweet sixteen and Billy Grimes the drover,
Has popped the question to me Ma, and wants to be my lover.
Tomorrow morn he says Mama he's coming here quite early,
To take a pleasant walk with me across the fields of barley."

"You shall not go my daughter dear
There ain't no use a-talkin'
You shall not go with Billy Grimes
Across the fields a-walkin'.
To think of his presumptions too
That dirty, ugly drover
I wonder where your pride had gone
To think of such a lover."

"Old Grimes is dead you know, Mama
And Billy is so lonely
Besides they say of Grimes's estate
That Billy is the only
Surviving heir to all that's left
And that they say is nearly
A good 10,000 dollars Ma,
At least 600 yearly."

"I did not hear my daughter dear
Your last remark quite clearly.
But Billy is a clever lad,
No doubt he loves you dearly.
Remember then tomorrow morn
To be up bright and early
And take a pleasant walk with him
Across the fields of barley."

This ballad was probably written by an N.C. Morse who published it under the title "Billy Grimes: The Drover" in Louisville, Kentucky, c.

1852. Evidently it was a very popular song, for the 1850s publication was the tenth edition of the ballad. Little more is known of Morse than that he also published a few other pieces of music, including a song titled " 'Tis Like Fairy Music Stealing" which probably appeared in the same year as "Billy Grimes." Morse's publication seemingly resolves a long-standing dispute among folksong specialists about whether the ballad is American or British in origin. Possibly, Morse was an American claiming a British song as his own, a not infrequent occurrence in the days when copyright enforcement was relatively lax. There is also the possibility that Morse was British, not American, although this is admittedly a weak likelihood. Still, the probabilities are that "Billy Grimes" is purely American in origin.

There are two basic forms of the ballad as found in the United States. In one the mother's worldliness is satirized, but in the other the drover turns the girl down because he doesn't care for either the girl's greed or that of her mother. In some texts Grimes is called a rover, probably because the singer is not familiar with the old way of conducting the cattle business. In most texts the protagonist is called Grimes although one Pennsylvania version has him named Will Ray.

The present text was collected July 8, 1947, by Byron Arnold from May Randlette Beck of Mobile, Alabama. Arnold, a native of Vancouver, Washington, was on the faculty of the University of Alabama from 1938 to 1948, during which time he did considerable collecting of folksongs. Some of the fruits of his work appeared in *Folksongs of Alabama* (1950), a work which is in the process of being republished. Arnold later moved to California, where he worked as an organist and choir director. He died on Christmas Day, 1971, in Oscoda, Michigan. Although he provided considerable information about some of his informants, Arnold told little about Mrs. Beck beyond the fact that she sang to her granddaughter, Nancy Beck Marty, with the microphone between them, an experience that Nancy apparently loved.

Four Nights Drunk or The Cabbage Head Song

*Alternate rhythm used in verses 1 - 4

SUNG BY SHEILA RICE BARNHILL, MARS HILL, NORTH CAROLINA, AT UNC WINTER FOLK
FESTIVAL, 1976. TRANSCRIPTION BY JULIE HENIGAN.

1. I came home the other night
As drunk as I could be,
Saw a hat on the rack
Where my hat oughtta be.

2. Said, come here, little wifey,
Explain this thing to me,
Why's the hat on the rack
Where my hat oughtta be?

3. You blind fool, you drunk old fool,
Can't you plainly see?
It's only a dishrag
Your granny gave to me.

4. I've traveled this whole world over,
A hundred times or more,
And a J.B. Stetson dishrag
I ain't never seen before.

5. I came home the other night
As drunk as I could be,
I saw a horse in the stable
Where my horse oughtta be.

6. Said, come here, little wifey,
Explain this thing to me;
Why's the horse here in the stable
Where my horse oughtta be?

7. You drunk fool, you blind old fool,
Can't you plainly see?
It's only a milk cow
Your granny gave to me.

8. I've traveled this whole world over,
A hundred times or more,
And a saddle on a milk cow
I ain't never seen before.

9. I came home drunk the other night
As drunk as I could be,
I saw some pants on the floor
Where my pants oughtta be.

10. Said, come here, little wifey,
And explain this thing to me,
Why's the pants here on the floor
Where my pants oughtta be?

11. You blind fool, you drunk old fool,
Can't you plainly see?
It's only a floursack
Your granny gave to me.

12. I've traveled this whole world over,
A hundred times or more,
And a zipper on a floursack
I ain't never seen before.

13. I came home the other night
As drunk as I could be,
I saw a head on the piller
Where my head oughtta be.

14. Said, come here, little wifey,
Explain this thing to me,
[Spoken: Why's the head on the piller
Where my head oughtta be?]

15. She said, you blind fool, you drunk old fool,
Can't you plainly see?
It's only a cabbage head
Your granny gave to me.

16. Well, I've traveled this whole world over,
A hundred times or more.
And a mustache on a cabbage head
I ain't never seen before.

Ole Lady

COLLECTED BY BECKY WILES, NOVEMBER 22, 1974, FROM MARY BROWN, LOUISIANA CORRECTIONAL INSTITUTE FOR WOMEN, ST. GABRIEL'S, LOUISIANA. TRANSCRIPTION BY DREW BEISSWENGER.

Ole lady, ole lady, whose ol' horse is dat,
Standin' at the gate where mine oughta be?
Old man, blind man, can't you ever see?
That jus' a milk cow my mama gave to me.

You may be right but I don' know,
I never seen a milk cow saddled up befo'.

Ole lady, ole lady, whose ol' hat is dat,
Layin' on the rack where mine oughta be?
Old man, blind man, can't you ever see?
That jus' a bonnet my mama gave to me.

You may be right but I don' know,
I never seen a bonnet wit' a hat crown on it befo'.

Ole lady, ole lady, whose ol' shoes are those
Layin' on the bed where mine oughta be?
Old man, blind man, can't you ever see?
That jus' some slippers my mama gave to me.

You may be right but I don' know,
I never seen slippers laceted up befo'.

Ole lady, ole lady, whose ol' head is that
Layin' in the bed where mine oughta be?
Old man, blind man, can't you ever see?
That just a sweet potato my mama gave to me.

You may be right but I don' know,
I never seen a sweet potato grow hair befo'.

This is possibly the most popular of the humorous Child ballads in America. Child catalogued it as number 274 under the title "Our Goodman," a title rarely used in America although there is one text collected in the United States that was called "Arrow Goodman," evidently a misunderstanding of the "Our" title. The most common titles in America refer to the number of days the man has been drunk, others include "The Adulteress," "A Blackguard Song," "Cario Girl," "Down Came the Old Man," "The Drunkard's Song," "Hobble and Bobble," "Home Came the Old Man," "I Called to My Loving Wife," "Kind Wife," "In Came the Gay Old Man," "Parson Jones," "Third Night of Married Life," "Three Nights Experience," "When I Came Home the Other Night," "Drunkard Blues," "The Drunken Fool," " Drunkard's Special," "Cabbage Head," "Mr. Goody Goody," "You Old Fool," "Saddle On a Milk Cow," "Old Man Brown," and several others very similar to these.

The first known printed version dates from the latter half of the eighteenth century but the ballad had probably been in existence for several decades by the time of this publication. As found in American tradition there are three story types, the first being that found in the first version given here. The other two types are identical except that in one the woman is entertaining three lovers and in the other the action occurs on three or four consecutive nights. The objects seen by the husband vary greatly and include a saddle, horse, boots, pistol, sword, wig, coat, hat, pants, and, of course, a man. Also varied are the items his wife tells him he is seeing, these include a cow, blanket, dishrag, spoon, floursack, petticoat, and, of course, a cabbage head.

There is less variation in the melodies generally used for this ballad. Most often it is 2/4 or 4/4 and versions often borrow melodic phrases from various other songs. This is particularly true in America where variants have been collected with traces of the melody of "Uncle Ned," "Oh, Susanna," "Ain't Goin' To Rain No More," "Polly-Wolly-Doodle," "Son of a Gambolier," "Jingle Bells," and "The Derby Ram" scattered throughout the song. Most authorities, however, agree with Bertrand Bronson who says that "all the singers were aiming at a roughly similar melodic ideal, in spite of the great divergences in their realizations of it."

"Our Goodman," or whatever title it is known by, is often not sung but instead recited as a dialogue. As might be expected, the story lends itself to ribaldry and there are many versions that are not intended for polite society or genteel company. Vance Randolph reported that Charles Ingenthron of Walnut Shade, Missouri, quit singing some verses of the ballad after joining the church. Arthur Kyle Davis concluded that "If ribald versions were collected and printed, no doubt every state would be represented" (*More Traditional Ballads From Virginia*, p. 30). Many of these versions, and for that matter several of the nonribald ones, are almost lacking balladic form, the song consisting of only portions of the dialogue.

The first version given here was recorded January 22, 1976, at the University of North Carolina Winter Folk Festival from the singing of Sheila Rice Barnhill, Mars Hill, North Carolina. Sheila, who at the time was in her early twenties, is the niece of folksinger Dellie Norton, one of several well-known traditional performers from Sodom, North Carolina. Although some of Sheila's repertoire comes from her relatives, she learned "Four Nights Drunk" or "The Cabbage Head Song" (she uses both titles for the ballad) from Mrs. Inez Chandler, a neighbor who died in 1981. Barnhill says "it is very important to me that the older folks be recognized for the valuable contribution they have made toward the preservation of the ballad tradition" (Personal letter to the author). Understandably, she is very proud of being the seventh generation of her family active in singing the old ballads.

The second version was collected November 22, 1974, by Becky Wiles from Mary Brown, an inmate at the Louisiana Correctional Institute for Women, St. Gabriel, Louisiana. Brown learned the song as a child from a neighbor of whom she was very fond. According to Wiles, "singing it now reminds her of those happier times when she was a child, the freest time of all."

Frog Went A-Courtin'

COLLECTED BY BYRON ARNOLD FROM CALLIE CRAVEN, GADSDEN, ALABAMA,
NOVEMBER 26, 1946. TRANSCRIPTION BY BYRON ARNOLD.

Frog went a courtin' and he did ride hmm, hmm
Frog went a courtin' and he did ride hmm, hmm
A sword and a pistol by his side hmm, hmm.

Took Miss Mousy on his knee hmm, hmm
Pray Miss Mousy will you marry me?
Hmm, hmm.

No, kind sir, I can't do that hmm, hmm
Unconsent of old Uncle Rat hmm, hmm.

Uncle Rat laughed on sugarfat sides hmm, hmm
To think his niece would be a bride hmm, hmm.

Uncle Rat he rode to town hmm, hmm
To get the wedding gown hmm, hmm.

Who do you reckon will make the wedding gown, hmm, hmm?
A very fine lady that lives in town hmm, hmm.

Where do you reckon the supper will be hmm, hmm?
Away down yonder in the holler tree, hmm, hmm.

What do you reckon they'll have for supper hmm, hmm?
Two black beans and not a speck of butter hmm, hmm.

First came in was a bumble bee hmm, hmm.
. . . . . .

Next came in was two black bugs hmm, hmm.
Cat came in and made a big spludge hmm, hmm.

Bride went tearing up the wall hmm, hmm.
Her foot slipped and she got a fall hmm, hmm.

Groom went swimming over the lake hmm, hmm.
He got·swallered by a big black snake hmm, hmm.

This is the end of one two three hmm, hmm.
A cat, rat, mouse and a bumble bee hmm, hmm.

This song is often considered a nursery ballad, but it is widely known by folksingers who consider it just a humorous song. It dates back at least to the sixteenth century and is possibly even older. The earliest known mention of it is in Wedderburn's *The Complaynt of Scotlande* where it is sung by the shepherds who call it "The Frog Cam to the Myl Dur (mill door)." It is generally believed that, like the Mother Goose rhymes which are also usually treated as children's material, the song originated as political satire. According to the theory, Queen Elizabeth I (1533–1603) nicknamed her suitors after animals: Sir Walter Raleigh was her "fish," Robert Dudley Leicester her "robin," the French ambassador Baron Jean de Simier her "ape," and the Duke of Alencon her "frog." Alencon's nickname probably resulted from the fact that his features had been disfigured by smallpox. While this thesis is not impossible, its credibility is greatly lessened by the fact the Alencon affair took place in the 1570s, over two decades after the first known appearance of the ballad. The song was entered in the Register of the London Company of Stationers, November 21, 1580, under the title "A Moste Strange Wedding of the Frogge and the Mouse." Most often it is known as "Frog (or Froggie) Went A-Courting" but is also known as "The Frog and the Mouse," "The Frog and the Mouse and the Bumblebee," "The Frog He Did A-Wooing Ride," "Uncle Rat," "The Froggie's Courtship," and "One, Two, Three." There are six different story types, all of them differentiated primarily on the basis of the refrain form. The three most popular in the United States are those with the "un-huh or hmmm," the "kemo-kimo," and the "Kitty alone and I" refrains, the first one being the most popular in the South.

In most versions the action begins with Frog setting out to court Miss Mousie with a sword and a pistol by his side. He goes to her house and proposes, and after that point the incidents vary from version to version. Most include the reply that she has to get her Uncle Rat's consent, discussion of the site and the food served at the wedding supper, and a series of verses referring to the procession of guests including a flea, a bumblebee, a toad, a duck, a black bug, a dog, a butterfly, and similar animals and insects. Many versions also include a snake who brings the action to an end when the newlyweds go swimming in the lake.

Many parodies of this song have been produced, a few of them entering folk tradition. Probably the most successful of these is one penned in the nineteenth century by British minstrel show performer

Sam Cowell, an artist who enjoyed a brief period of popularity in America during the 1850s. His parody tells of "an old frog who lived in the spring/he was so hoarse he couldn't sing." Possibly Cowell's parody was a satire ridiculing some specific person, but if so he has not been identified.

The song has appeared on several commercial recordings, a situation that certainly has aided its popularity. But even without such help it would still be widely popular, for despite frequent printings and recordings it also is very much alive in oral tradition. Indeed, it may be one of the very few traditional ballads that is known throughout the entire United States. The present text was collected November 26, 1946, by Byron Arnold from Callie Craven, Gadsden, Alabama. For more information about Arnold and Craven see the notes for "Barb'ry Allen" in Volume I.

The Girl That Wore A Waterfall

COLLECTED MAY 22, 1981, BY W.K. MCNEIL FROM LEE FINIS CAMERON "TIP" MCKINNEY,
SEARCY, ARKANSAS. TRANSCRIPTION BY W.K. MCNEIL.

Come all of you that's been in love,
O sympathize with me,
For I have loved the fairest girl
That ever you did see,
Her age it was but seventeen,
She's a figger fair an' tall,
She was a handsome creature
And she wore a waterfall.

The first time I ever saw her
I never shall forget.
I went into a drygoods store
Some handkerchiefs to get.
She stood behind the counter
And her glance did on me fall,
I never seen such a face so fair
And such a waterfall.

I met her at a picnic party
I met her after that,
We quickly introduced ourselves,
And I had a pleasant chat.
While walking along I saw her home,
I told her we'd never part,
And when she asked me to come in
I seen she'd won my heart.

While sitting there I thought I heard
A footstep in the hall.
All sorts of colors turned the girl
That wore that waterfall.
A great big man about six foot tall
Come stalking through the room,
An' while he seen me there
So he began to fume.

Before I'd time to say a word
The feller at me flew
An' while the maiden held me down
He beat me black an' blue.
When I got up I found I'd lost
Watch, money, chain and all,
And I've never been about another girl since
That wore a waterfall.

This tragic tale of a man who placed too much faith in a girl wearing a stylish hairdo is of unknown origin but is generally believed to come from the music hall stage. Nevertheless, stylistically it shares some relationship to British broadside balladry. A waterfall, which is a mass of artificially curled hair worn at the back of the head and arranged about a set of false hair called a "rat," first became popular in the United States in the 1840s, enjoying a vogue that lasted approximately twenty years and has been revived periodically since. Thus, the song probably dates from the immediate pre–Civil War era. It has been reported by folksong collectors from Virginia, Kentucky, Iowa, Nebraska, North Carolina, and Missouri, but is probably more widely known than these references indicate because collectors often don't report items thought to be of stage origin.

The version given here is from the singing of Lee Finis Cameron McKinney of Searcy, Arkansas. Mr. McKinney is known to everyone as "Tip," a nickname he acquired in childhood, and is locally famed as the lead singer of Pope's Arkansas Mountaineers, a string band that made eight sides for the old Victor label in 1928. Although in his eighty-fourth year at the time of collection, he still had a strong voice and got more enjoyment from singing than anyone else I have ever recorded. A smile spread across his face whenever he started singing, and he delivered each vocal with the enthusiasm and spirit of a man many decades his junior.

Tip was born in 1897 near the community of Rosebud, Arkansas. He was the youngest of ten children, most of whom were musicians, and he recalls that his father, Guy McKinney, was a fine ballad singer. During

Tip's youth the entire family frequently performed at local functions; he remembers being especially fond of comic songs. Apparently this love of humor never abated, for three of the eight sides he recorded with Pope's Arkansas Mountaineers were comedy numbers. His rendition of "I'm Old But I'm Awfully Tough" is the title piece for an excellent album of Ozark music recorded by the Missouri Friends of the Folk Arts.

Tip McKinney recalls very well where he learned "The Girl That Wore a Waterfall." It was during the early years of this century at a party held in honor of three-time Arkansas governor Jeff Davis (1862–1913). A teenage girl sang the number and McKinney liked it so well he immediately learned it. As he puts it, "I used to be able to learn songs quick like that but I can't no more."

I Wish I Was Single Again

COLLECTED BY BYRON ARNOLD FROM MYRTLE LOVE HESTER, FLORENCE, ALABAMA,
NO DATE GIVEN BUT PROBABLY 1945. TRANSCRIPTION BY BYRON ARNOLD.

I wish I was single again, again
I wish I was single again;
For when I was single my pockets did jingle;
So I wish I was single again.

I married me a wife oh then, oh then,
I married me a wife oh then;
I married me a wife and I loved her for my life
But I wished I was single again.

She beat me, she banged me, oh then, oh then,
She beat me, she banged me, oh then,
She beat me, she banged me, she swore she would hang me,
So I wished I was single again.

She spun the rope, oh then, oh then,
She spun the rope, oh then,
She spun the rope my neck for to choke,
So I wished I was single again.

She tied it to the joist, oh then, oh then,
She tied it to the joist, oh then,
But the rope it did break and my neck did escape,
But I wished I was single again.

So then she died, oh then, oh then,
So then she died, oh then,
So then she died and I laughed till I cried,
But I wished I was single again.

I married me another, oh then, oh then,
I married me another, oh then,
I married me another; she was the devil's grandmother.
Oh I wished I was single again.

I Wish I Were Single Again

WORDS AND MUSIC BY JAMES C. BECKEL. 1871.

I wish I were single, O then, O then!
I wish I were single, O then!
When I was single my pockets did jingle
And I wish I were single again.

When I was single, oh then, oh then!
When I was single, oh then!
I liv'd at my ease and I went where I pleas'd
And I wish I were single again.

I married a wife, oh then, oh then!
I married a wife, oh then!
I married a wife, she's the plague of my life,
And I wish I were single again.

And now I am married, oh! then, oh! then!
And now I am married, oh! then!
If I go anywhere, my wife's sure to be there,
And I wish I were single again.

When my wife died, oh! then, oh! then!
When my wife died, oh! then!
When my wife died, I'll be hanged if I cried,
So glad to be single again.

I went to the funeral, oh! then, oh! then!
I went to the funeral, oh! then!
The music did play, and I danced all the way,
So glad to be single again.

I married another, oh! then, oh! then!
I married another, oh! then!
I married another, she's worse than the tother!
And I wish I were single again.

Now all ye young men, oh! then, oh! then!
Now all ye young men, oh! then!
Be kind to your first, or the last will prove worse!
And you'll wish for the old one again.

Authorship of this ballad is disputed. According to Mike Yates in his brochure notes for Topic album 12TS324 *Round Rye Bay for More*, a version appeared in the *Westminster Drollery* (1672), but there are several other claims of more recent vintage. It was printed as one of *Sam Cowell's 120 Comic Songs* (c. 1850) and in 1871 it was credited to James C. Beckel, who copyrighted it as "I Wish I Were Single Again." Beckel, a fairly prolific songwriter, had a number of minor successes including "When Hope Is Chidden" (late 1830s), "Bonny Belle of Sante Fe" (1855), and "Katy Darling" (early 1860s), but "I Wish I Were Single Again" was easily his biggest hit; ironically it was not an original but merely an arrangement of an older song. Beckel's version, with some minor changes, is, however, the one generally found in the repertoires of twentieth-century folksingers.

Writing in 1914, Henry M. Belden, the Missouri folksong scholar, said that a Kansas ballad-singer named George Meeks claimed authorship of the ballad. Given what is known of the song's previous history, Meeks's claim can't be taken seriously. The essential idea of this song is found in a related piece titled "I'm Satisfied" that was written by a north Georgia fiddler, Gid Tanner. Tanner (1885–1960) was nominally the leader of the Skillet Lickers, one of the most important and long-lived early country recording acts. "I'm Satisfied" is in the form of a dialogue between man and wife, with the alternating voices imitated in the refrain which consists of the title repeated twice.

"I Wish I Was Single Again" has been collected primarily from southern traditional singers but has also been reported from Kansas, Wyoming, Nebraska, Utah, Missouri, Oklahoma, Ohio, and Michigan. The piece has also appeared on several commercial records. All of these versions feature the lament for bachelorhood, description of mistreatment by the wife, her death, and the narrator's marriage to a second wife who proves to be worse than the first. There are several variations and expansions on these basic elements; few versions, however, extend beyond ten stanzas. The moral found in Beckel's eighth verse has disappeared from most American texts.

The present version was collected probably in 1945 (the exact date of collection isn't given) by Byron Arnold from Myrtle Love Hester, Florence, Alabama. Although Hester was a recent graduate of Florence State Teachers College at the time Arnold recorded her songs, she was nearing middle age and had raised a family. The oldest of eight daughters and one son of an Alabama minister, Hester learned most of her songs from her father and grandmother. A jovial woman, Hester was a very willing informant who kept Arnold laughing during much of the time he worked with her.

Old Judge Duffy

COLLECTED MARCH 16, 1978, BY W.K. MCNEIL FROM CLEM ADAMS, YELLVILLE, ARKANSAS. TRANSCRIPTION BY DREW BEISSWENGER.

Old John Martin Duffy was judge in our court
In a small ranching town in the West;
Although he knew nothing about rules of the law,
For judge he was one of the best.

One night in the winter a murder occurred,
And our blacksmith accused of the crime.
They caught him red-handed and though he'd two trials,
The verdict was guilty each time.

Now he was the only good blacksmith we had,
And we wanted to spare him his life,
So Duffy rose up in the court like a lord,
And with these words he settled the strife:

"I move we discharge him, we need him in town,"
Then spoke out the words that have gained him renown:
"We've two Chinese laundrymen, everyone knows,
Why not save the poor blacksmith and hang one of those?"

Although the particular incident described in "Old Judge Duffy" may be fictitious the situation it describes is very realistic. Chinese laborers were very prominent in early Western towns, particularly in those areas primarily noted for gold mining. In some cases the bulk of the population consisted of Asiatic laborers. While in some communities these people became leading citizens, in others they were much abused and denied even basic freedoms and dignities. A common practice in mining communities ("Old Judge Duffy" is usually set in a mining town) was to hire a gang of Chinese laborers to work in the mines and then not pay them. When the Chinese began to complain about their pay, a convenient explosion was arranged in order to eliminate the problem.

Such heartless treatment of minorities is characteristic of most periods of American settlement and there are many folksongs dealing with such situations from the minority viewpoint. Here, though, the perspective is that of the majority group, and the existing prejudices are treated in a humorous light. The ballad, then, is historically ethnically accurate and its singers often claim it describes an actual event. For example, folklorist Barre Toelken was told by various informants that the incident actually occurred in Florence, Idaho; Jacksonville, Oregon; and near Nespelem, Washington. In the absence of supporting proof these claims should not be taken too seriously because it is a relatively common practice among American folksingers to localize ballads.

The best guess is that the song originated in either the music hall or Tin Pan Alley during the late nineteenth century and from that source made its way to the folk repertoire. It is believed that the number was widely sung in the American West at the turn of the century. There is, however, little doubt that George Gobel (1919–) played a considerable role in the song's dissemination, for as a child star on the WLS National Barn Dance he frequently performed the song. Although it was one of his most popular numbers, he never recorded the piece.

The version given here was collected from Clem Adams of Yellville, Arkansas, March 16, 1978. A very good old-time guitarist and singer, Adams moved to the Ozarks in 1973 from his native Illinois. Back in the 1930s he and his brother Vince performed as an old-time duet singing over stations in northern Illinois and southern Wisconsin as "The Adams Brothers, Twelve Feet of Harmony" (a reference to their height; both were six-footers). On several occasions they appeared on the influential WLS National Barn Dance from Chicago. Clem still remembers and sings many of the numbers they used to perform, one of them being "Old Judge Duffy."

The Rattlesnake Song

COLLECTED BY W.K. MCNEIL FROM NOBLE COWDEN, CUSHMAN, ARKANSAS, IN
DECEMBER 1979. TRANSCRIPTION BY W.K. MCNEIL.

Oh, Johnny dear, don't you go
Down in the meadow for to mow,
Ra tinga ling day, ra tinga ling day,
Ra tinga ling linga tinga ling day.

Oh, Molly dear, don't you know
Father's meadow and it must be mowed
Ra tinga ling day, ra tinga ling day,
Ra tinga ling linga tinga ling day.

He hadn't mowed around the field,
Rattlesnake bit him on the heel,
Ra tinga ling day, ra tinga ling day,
Tinga ling linga tinga ling day.

They carried him home to Molly dear,
Don't you know she felt right queer.
Ra tinga ling day, ra tinga ling day,
Ra tinga ling linga tinga ling day.

Come all my friends and warning take,
Never get bit by a rattler snake.
Ra tinga ling day, ra tinga ling day,
Ra tinga ling linga tinga ling day.

If you do I'm telling you,
Lots of trouble you'll get into.
Ra tinga ling day, ra tinga ling day,
Ra tinga ling linga tinga ling day.

This song, originally known as "Springfield Mountain," is certainly
among the oldest native American ballads still in folk tradition. It is
thought to deal with the death of one Timothy Myrick of Wilbraham,

Massachusetts, formerly Springfield Mountain, who expired from a snakebite in Farmington, Connecticut, August 7, 1761. At some point in time the serious ballad became converted into a comic ballad, so today both traditions exist simultaneously. Phillips Barry, who made an extensive study of this song, suggests that each of the two ballad types has several subtypes. He was able to trace the comic ballads back to 1836, with the serious song only dating back to 1849. G. Malcolm Laws feels that Barry is in error on this point and suggests that the original ballad was composed locally and soon after the tragedy it recounts.

Considering its widespread distribution, this ballad has remarkably few titles. By far the most popular is "Springfield Mountain" but "The Shrattledum Snake" and "The Rattlesnake Song" are other traditional titles. Melodically the serious ballad maintains a somber mood while the comic versions have a quicker tempo and lighter mood. Like most of the comic ballads, the one given here contains a nonsense refrain and achieves much of its effect by exaggerating a basically tragic story. In some versions of the ballad the protagonist is referred to merely as "a likely youth" or some similar description. Most texts do supply him with a name, generally John or Johnny but never Timothy; Myrick, however, is found in several versions. Molly, Sally, or Sal are the names generally given the woman, but in some texts she is not named. Barry thought the woman's name came from the comic tradition and was the work of professional songwriters.

The version given here was collected in December 1979 by W.K. McNeil from the singing of Noble Cowden of Cushman, Arkansas. For more information about Mrs. Cowden see the notes to "The House Carpenter's Wife."

Three Jolly Welshmen

COLLECTED JANUARY 26, 1954, BY GEORGE W. BOSWELL FROM MRS. ANNIE
STEVENSON, CLARKSVILLE, TENNESSEE. TRANSCRIPTION BY GEORGE W. BOSWELL.

Three jolly Welshmen and jolly boys were they,
They went a-hunting on St. Patrick's Day.
Look a-there now!

They hunted and they whooped, and the first thing they did find
Was a barn in a meadow, and that they left behind.
Look a-there now!

One said it was a barn, and the other he said nay,
One said it was a haystack with the top blown away.
Look a-there now!

They hunted and they whooped, and the next thing they did find
Was a frog in the well, and that they left behind.
Look a-there now!

One said it was a frog, and the other he said nay,
One said it was a jaybird with his feathers washed away.
Look a-there now!

They hunted and they whooped, and the next thing they did find
Was a pig in the lane and that they left behind.
Look a-there now!

One said it was a pig, and the other he said nay,
One said it was an elephant with its trunk cut away.
Look a-there now!

They hunted and they whooped and the next thing they did find
Was a babe in the woods and that they left behind.
Look a-there now!

One said it was a babe, and the other he said nay,
One said it was a monkey with the tail cut away.
Look a-there now!

They hunted and they whooped, and the next thing they did find
Was the moon in the elements and that they left behind.
Look a-there now!

One said it was the moon, the other he said nay,
One said it was a cheese with a half cut away.
Look a-there now!

They hunted and they whooped, and the next thing they did find
Was a woman in the kitchen and that they left behind.
Look a-there now!

One said it was a woman, and the other he said nay,
One said it was an angel with the wings cut away.
Look a-there now!

They hunted and they whooped, and the next thing they did find
Was an owl in an ivy bush and that they left behind.
Look a-there now!

One said it was an owl, and the other he said nay,
One said it was the Devil, and they all ran away.
Look a-there now!

    The first recorded appearance of this ballad occurred in a play of which Shakespeare wrote a part. In Act III, Scene 5, of *The Two Noble Kinsmen,* the jailer's crazed daughter sings:

There was three fools, fell out about an howlet:
The one sed it was an owl
The other he sed nay,
The third he sed it was a hawk, and her bels were cut away.

A stanza of it was also sung in William Davenant's comedy *The Rivals* (1668). So by the seventeenth century the ballad was a familiar one, which soon became known far and wide. It became popular in Ireland and in the nineteenth century was reportedly sung in a circus by a group of Alabama Negroes. In America it has also been reported from folk tradition in Maine, Vermont, North Carolina, Missouri, Virginia, Massachusetts, and Ohio. In the mid-1840s it became a popular song as performed by the Hutchinson Family, one of the leading popular singing groups of that era.

    In addition to "Three Jolly Welshmen" the ballad is also known as "The Fox Chase," "The Fox Hunt," "Lookey There," "We Hunted and We Halloed," "Come All Ye Jolly Sportsmen," "We Hooped and We Hollered," and "Cape Ann" (the title of the Hutchinson Family version), among others. An influential version titled "Three Men Went A-Hunting" was recorded in the 1920s by Byrd Moore's Hot Shots. Moore, a Norton,

Virginia, barber, changed the last verse explaining why the men ran away into a comic line about the town they were playing. Moore's lyrics referred to the three men as a Scotsman, Irishman, and Welshman; other texts refer to them as an Englishman, Scotchman, and Irishman, or, as in the case with the text given here, three Welshmen.

The version given here was collected January 26, 1954, by George W. Boswell from Mrs. Annie Stevenson in Clarksville, Tennessee. Mrs. Stevenson had the song from her father, F. Ross McCuddy, who was born in Pembroke, Kentucky, in 1848. Boswell was at the time a teacher at Austin Peay State College in Clarksville.

The Wife in Wether's Skin—Dandoo!

COLLECTED BY GEORGE FOSS FROM ERNEST BYRD, CULLOWHEE, NORTH CAROLINA, 1962. TRANSCRIBED BY GEORGE FOSS.

> There was an old man who lived in the West,
>> Dandoo,
> There was an old man who lived in the West,
>> To my clash a' my klingo,
> There was an old man who lived in the West,
> He married him a wife which he thought the best,
>> Lingarum, lingorum, smikaroarum, kerrymingorum,
>> To my clash a' my klingo.

Now this good man came from his plow,
    Dandoo,
Now this good man came from his plow,
    To my clash a' my klingo,
Now this good man came from his plow,
"Oh wife, is breakfast ready now?"
        Lingarum, lingorum, smikaroarum, kerrymingorum,
        To my clash a' klingo.

"There's a piece of bread upon the shelf."
    Dandoo,
"There's a piece of bread upon the shelf."
    To my clash a' my klingo,
"There's a piece of bread upon the shelf.
If you want any more, you can get it yourself."
        Lingarum, lingorum, smikaroarum, kerrymingorum,
        To my clash a' my klingo.

Now this good man went out to his sheep pen.
    Dandoo,
Now this good man went out to his sheep pen.
    To my clash a' my klingo.
Now this good man went out to his sheep pen,
He grabbed him up an old sheep skin.
        Lingarum, lingorum, smikaroarum, kerrymingorum,
        To my clash a' my klingo.

He threw that skin 'round his wife's back,
    Dandoo,
He threw that skin 'round his wife's back,
    To my clash a' my klingo,
He threw that skin 'round his wife's back,
And with a big stick he went whickety-whack.
        Lingarum, lingorum, smikaroarum, kerrymingorum,
        To my clash a' my klingo.

"I'll tell my neighbors, I'll tell my kin."
    Dandoo,
"I'll tell my neighbors, I'll tell my kin."
    To my clash a' my klingo.
"I'll tell my neighbors, I'll tell my kin
That you beat me up with a big hickory limb."
        Lingarum, lingorum, smikaroarum, kerrymingorum,
        To my clash a' my klingo.

"Go tell your neighbors, go tell your kin."
    Dandoo,
"Go tell your neighbors, go tell your kin."
    To my clash a' my klingo.
"Go tell your neighbors, go tell your kin.
I was only tanning my old sheep skin."
    Lingarum, lingorum, smikaroarum, kerrymingorum,
    To my clash a' my klingo.

Ever since that time she had been a good wife,
    Dandoo,
Ever since that time she had been a good wife,
    To my clash a' my klingo,
Ever since that time she has been a good wife,
And I hope she'll be all the rest of her life.
    Lingarum, lingorum, smikaroarum, kerrymingorum,
    To my clash a' my klingo.

Geely Don Mac Kling Go

COLLECTED BY MARION TAYLOR PAGE FROM NANCY MCCUDDY STEVENSON, ST. BETHLEHEM, TENNESSEE. EXACT DATE OF COLLECTION NOT GIVEN BUT WAS SOMETIME BETWEEN 1953 AND 1955. TRANSCRIBED BY MARION TAYLOR PAGE.

There was a man lived in the west,
    Geely don mac kling go.
There was a man lived in the west.
He had a wife none of the best.
        Like a larum clen darum,
        Geely don mac kling go.

His wife would neither cook nor wash,
    Geely don mac kling go.
His wife would neither cook nor wash,
For fear she would make a slosh.
        Like a larum clen darum,
        Geely don mac kling go.

His wife would neither card nor spin,
    Geely don mac kling go.
His wife would neither card nor spin,
For fear she'd spoil her wedding ring.
        Like a larum clen darum,
        Geely don mac kling go.

This good man went to his sheep fold,
    Geely don mac kling go.
This good man went to his sheep fold,
And there he killed a wether bold.
        Like a larum clen darum,
        Geely don mac kling go.

He put the skin on his wife's back,
    Geely don mac kling go.
He put the skin on his wife's back,
And with a stick went whickety whack.
        Like a larum clen darum,
        Geely don mac kling go.

His wife would then both cook and wash,
    Geely don mac kling go.
His wife would then both cook and wash,
And never fear'f she'd make a slosh.
    Like a larum clen darum,
    Geely don mac kling go.

His wife would then both card and spin,
    Geely don mac kling go.
His wife would then both card and spin,
Nor fear'f she'd spoil her wedding ring.
    Like a larum clen darum,
    Geely don mac kling go.

These two ballads are versions of Child 277, "The Wife Wrapt In Wether's Skin." The earliest reports of this ballad are from the late eighteenth century but it is generally thought to be derived from the traditional tale *The Wife Lapped in Morrel's Skin,* which was known at least as early as the first half of the sixteenth century. In America the ballad has been collected in Florida, Maine, Missouri, Indiana, Colorado, North Carolina, New York, West Virginia, Virginia, Vermont, Tennessee, Utah, Mississippi, Pennsylvania, Texas, Nebraska, Kentucky, Oklahoma, and Arkansas, and it has also been reported from Nova Scotia. Thus it is certainly one of the more popular Child ballads in America. It is known by numerous titles including "Bandoo," "Dandoo," "Dan-Doodle-Dan," "Dindo-Dan," "Gentle Fair Ginny," "Gentle Virginia," "Jennifer Gently," "Jenny Flow," "Gentle Rosemary," "John Dobber," "Jock O McKee," "Kitty Lorn," "Nickety, Nackety," "Old Man Come In from his Plow," "The Old Man in the West," "The Old Sheepskin," "Robin He's Gone to the Woods," "The Scolding Wife," "Sweet Robin," "The Wee Cooper o' Fife," "Old Wetherskin," "Lazy Woman," and the titles used here.

There are three story types of this ballad that are common in American folk tradition. The first is the story given in the two texts presented here; a second involves the old man running away in the end, while a third omits the "wether's skin"; the man merely beats his wife to reform her. There are several varied refrains found in American versions of this ballad, the most common being the "dandoo-clish ma clingo" type found in the South and Midwest, and the "rosemary-thyme" type found in the South and Northeast.

The first of the two versions given here was collected in 1962 by George Foss from Ernest Byrd, Cullowhee, North Carolina. Byrd was a member of the administration of Western Carolina University who had a large repertoire of traditional songs he learned in his childhood. The second version was collected between 1953 and 1955 by Marion Taylor

Page from Nancy McCuddy Stevenson, St. Bethlehem, Tennessee. For more information about Stevenson see the notes to "Lord Lovel."

Willy Weaver

stanza 4 same as others except measures 7-8

COLLECTED BY VIRGIL L. STURGILL FROM JAMES S. LANE, ENKA, NORTH CAROLINA, DATE NOT GIVEN BUT PROBABLY 1940S OR 1950S. TRANSCRIBED BY DANIEL W. PATTERSON.

"Mammy, Mammy, now I'm married,
Single life I wish I'd tarried,
For the women they do swear
That the britches they do wear."

"She don't lie and she don't tatter.
She don't sigh and she don't flatter,
But she does to the tavern go,
'Long with Willy Weaver, O."

"Son, oh Son, oh what's the matter?
Does she lie and does she tatter?
Does she to the tavern go,
'Long with Willy Weaver, O."

He run home all in a wonder,
Beat on the door just like thunder.
"Who is there, who is here,
Staying all night with my dear?"

Into the hall he did enter.
Into the hall he did vent're.
Searched the walls and chambers round—
Nobody there to be found.

Up the chimney he was a-gazing.
Up the chimney he was amazing.
Thar he spied the wretched soul,
A-setting astraddle of the pot-rack pole.

He built on a roaring fury.
She cried out, "Oh my deary,
Bring him down and spare his life,
For he has a lawful wife!"

Up he re'ched and down he fetched him.
Like a raccoon dog he sheck him.
Beat his back and belly red—
Now poor Willy Weaver's dead.

This tale of a triangular situation was known in England and Scotland in the late eighteenth century as attested by its publication on a broadside of the 1790s. The song was also included in a chapbook (a small booklet usually of eight to twenty-four pages, illustrated on the title page by a woodcut, containing verse or prose designed for a popular audience, and sold for a small sum by peddlers) printed between 1823 and 1829. It also appeared on numerous broadsides, the earliest known American ones dating from c. 1814. The ballad is generally called "Will the Weaver" but on at least one occasion was collected as "Bill the Weaver." It has been recorded from traditional singers in Indiana, Nova Scotia, and Pennsylvania, but has primarily been found in the South, a fact that may merely represent more active collecting in this region and possibly has nothing to do with greater popularity in the South than elsewhere.

Henry W. Shoemaker suggests that the ballad is derived from "Gil Morrice" (Child 83), not an impossibility but no certainty either. In "Gil Morrice" it is a boy, who turns out to be the woman's son, who is killed, definitely a far different situation than the story related here. "Will the Weaver" should not be confused with "Willy the Weeper," an entirely different song reported by Carl Sandburg in *The American Songbag*.

The present text was collected by Virgil L. Sturgill from James S. Lane, Enka, North Carolina, at an uncertain date but probably in the early 1950s. Lane was well known locally for his singing and Sturgill was himself a frequent performer at various folk festivals. Both men are now deceased.

Murder Ballads

Little Marian Parker

COLLECTED JUNE 25, 1979, BY W.K. MCNEIL FROM REBECCA SIMMONS, SHIRLEY, ARKANSAS. TRANSCRIPTION BY W.K. MCNEIL.

Away out in California
Lived a family bright and gay.
There were planning for their Christmas
Not very far away.

When along came a murderous stealer
With a heart as hard as stone,
Took little Marian Parker
Away from friends and home.

He took her to the movies,
He gave her candy too.
He told her every promise
That he would be kind and true.

I only want the money
That your daddy can give.
And if he'll give the money
His little child can live.

But late in the evening
She found that he had lied,
For before the evening sunset
The little child had died.

O there is a great commandment
Thou shalt not kill,
And those who do not heed it
Must suffer unto God's will.

This song should be a warning
To parents far and near.
You can't guide too closely
The ones you love so dear.

The story behind this ballad began on December 14, 1927, when nineteen-year-old William Edward Hickman went to a public school in Los Angeles and told the teacher that eleven-year-old Marian Parker's father had been injured in an automobile accident and wanted his daughter to come home. Marian left with Hickman and three days later, on December 17, her father received notes demanding a huge ransom fee. Wishing to get his daughter back alive, Mr. Parker took the fifteen $100 bills demanded and handed them over to Hickman. After receiving the ransom Hickman drove away. As he went, he tossed a part of Marian's body at the distraught father's feet. Immediately a manhunt began for Hickman, but it was several days before he was found. When he was caught, Hickman was tried and found guilty of kidnapping and first-degree murder. He was convicted on February 9, 1928, and executed at San Quentin on October 19 of that year.

Perhaps because of the victim's age the Parker case achieved nation-wide interest. People eagerly read about the search for the kidnapper and his subsequent trial, conviction, and execution. This situation was not lost on the Oswego, Kansas, songwriter Carson J. Robison (1890–1957), who composed a ballad on the topic that was recorded in 1928 by Marion Try Slaughter (1883–1948), a singer whose best known of 250 pseudonyms was Vernon Dalhart. Eventually three other ballads, two of them titled "Marian Parker" and the third titled "Edward Hickman," about the case appeared. Two of these, the Hickman song and one of the Parker ones, are the work of Andrew Jenkins (1885–1956), a prolific country songwriter-composer of the 1920s. His efforts apparently were written later than Robison's for they both mention the death sentence whereas Robison's text fails to comment about what happened to the killer.

Ballads about Marian Parker have rarely been reported by folksong collectors, but that should not be taken as evidence of their lack of popularity with traditional singers. Traditionally, folksong specialists have avoided those pieces of relatively current vintage, especially if they could be traced back to a specific recording or songwriter. Previously the Robison version of "Little Marian Parker" has been reported from traditional sources only in Utah, Iowa, Oregon, New York, and North Carolina. The present text is proof that the song also is known and sung in the Ozarks. This version was recorded by W.K. McNeil from the singing of Rebecca Simmons of Shirley, Arkansas, in 1979. Mrs. Simmons had a fairly large repertoire but was not in particularly good voice on the day of the recording because of a cold. She no longer recalls where she learned the song but is certain that it did not come from a record. The fact that her version differs somewhat from any recorded version supports her view.

Little Mary Fagan

AS SUNG BY MRS. ARTIE WAGGONER OF CRESTON, LOUISIANA

Little Mary Fagan
She went to town one day.
She went to the pencil factory
To get her little pay.

Leo Benton met her
With a brutal heart we know.
He smiled and said, "Little Mary
You'll go home no more."

He sneaked along behind her
Until she reached the little room.
He laughed and said, "Little Mary
You've met your fatal doom."

Jim Newt he was the watchman
And when he turned the key
Away down in the basement
Little Mary he could see.

He called out for the policemen
Whose names I do not know.
They came to the pencil factory
And told Newt he must go.

Her mother is a-weeping;
She weeps from night til day.
She prays to meet her baby
In a better world someday.

Judge Long he passed the sentence,
You bet he did not fail.
Oh, when he passed the sentence
To send that brute to jail.

Come you good people
Wherever you may be.
Supposing little Mary
Had belonged to you or me.

Little Mary Phagan

AS RECALLED BY MRS. REBA CHEYNE OF FORT SMITH, ARKANSAS

Little Mary Phagan,
She went to town one day,
She went to the pencil factory,
To draw her weekly pay.

She left her home at seven,
She kissed her mother goodbye,
(This line is forgotten)
That she was going to die.

Leo Frank he met her,
What a cruel heart you know.
He laughed and said, "Little Mary,
You won't go home anymore."

The tears rolled down her rosy cheeks,
The blood fled down her back.
She remembered telling her mother,
What time she would be back.

Now Little Mary's in Heaven,
And Leo Frank's in jail,
Waiting for the day to come,
When he can tell his tale.

The murder of Mary Fagan was perhaps the most widely reported Southern crime of the first half of the twentieth century. Many of the elements in this case—sex, anti-Semitism, and lynching—sound as if they were taken from a pot-boiler novel but, unfortunately, they are all true. The dramatic possibilities of the incident have not been ignored, for it has inspired at least one movie and two songs. What is the story that has received all of this attention?

On Sunday, April 27, 1913, Newt Lee, nightwatchman of the National Pencil Factory, discovered the body of Mary Phagan, a thirteen-year-old employee of the company, lying on a pile of cinders in the basement of the Georgia factory. The corpse was badly bruised, several fingers were broken, and the girl had been raped. Evidence later compiled revealed that at the time of death only Leo Max Frank (1884–1915), superintendent of the factory, and Jim Conley (1886–1962), a Negro janitor, were in the building. Conley was found washing blood from his shirt and arrested on suspicion of murder; strangely, no one even bothered to test the blood stains on the shirt. Despite the oversight, Conley soon was released because he told a fantastic story blaming Leo Frank. According to this tale the superintendent committed the crime, and Conley was only an accomplice who helped him get rid of the body. After this testimony Frank was arrested and charged with murder. A short time later Frank was convicted and sentenced to death while Conley received a year's labor on the chain gang.

Throughout the trial a virulent wave of anti-Semitism, fostered not only by some papers but by a number of prominent citizens including Tom Watson, made the likelihood of a fair trial for Frank, a Jew, unlikely. Governor John M. Slaton recognized the prejudicial nature of the proceedings and after lengthy hearings commuted Frank's death sentence to life imprisonment. The convicted man was sent to the state prison at Milledgeville and, although he could not have known it, had only a few weeks to live. A portent of things to come occurred just four weeks after his arrival in Milledgeville. One night while Frank was sleeping, a fellow convict, William Creen, attempted to slash his throat with a butcher knife. This attack was foiled but not before Creen had opened a seven-and-a-half-inch wound in his victim's throat. Creen said he had been called "from on high" to murder the Jew and also explained that he had tried to kill Frank in order to prevent other prisoners from being harmed, should an attempt be made to storm the prison and abduct its most notorious inmate. Many Georgians sent petitions to then Governor Nathaniel Harris asking that Creen be pardoned as a reward for his deed.

The abduction Creen referred to had been in the planning stage ever since Slaton's commutation. Then, on August 16, 1915, twenty-five of the "best citizens" of Marietta, Mary Phagan's home town, put the scheme into effect. They broke into the jail at Milledgeville, kidnapped Frank, and lynched him. But the plan did not go smoothly. Some of the mob began to doubt that Frank was guilty of the crime for which he was convicted and at least one member mutinied, urged the others to return Frank to prison, and refused to take part in the execution. But the majority stood their ground and carried out their grisly deed.

According to legend the lynchers sang a ballad about Mary Phagan just before executing Frank. Certainly such a song was in existence, although it was not printed before 1918. In that year Franklyn Bliss Snyder published in the *Journal of American Folklore* "Leo Frank and Mary Phagan" that he collected from a young Georgia singer "who claimed to have heard several variants from a number of other singers." One year later, in 1919, Nancy Maxwell collected a version of "Little Mary Phagan" in Hazelwood, North Carolina, a small town about 250 miles north of Atlanta. During the 1920s a number of commercial recordings of the piece appeared. Marion Try Slaughter (1883–1948) recorded it at least three times, in each instance under a pseudonym. On the Romeo label he is listed as Vernon Dalhart, his most famous pseudonym; for Columbia he is Al Craver, and for Okeh, Tobe Little. Rosa Lee Carson, the daughter of Fiddlin' John Carson (1868–1949), also recorded the song. This ballad is relatively common in oral tradition.

A second song about the Phagan case also appeared on records but has not, to my knowledge, ever been reported from field collections of folksongs. First, a version by Fiddlin' John Carson was released under the title "The Grave of Little Mary Phagan" in 1926. A year later, in 1927, a second version by Earl Johnson and his Clodhoppers was released as 'The Little Grave in Georgia." Both of these pieces are directly traceable to an Irish song usually called "Over the Mountain," the title used by Uncle Dave Macon (1870–1952) for his 1929 record of this version. Each of these three recordings and the extant versions of the other ballad took the view that Frank was guilty.

For some years the Phagan case remained a sensitive issue in Georgia. As late as 1942 a historian was denied access to records concerning Frank on the grounds that any investigation would arouse too many bad feelings. Nevertheless, in 1936 Ward Greene published a book called *Death in the Deep South* based on the Phagan murder. A year later, in 1937, Greene's book was adapted into a successful movie, "They Won't Forget," starring Claude Rains. This feature is now best remembered for marking the debut of Lana Turner, then a busty teenager and totally inappropriate in the Phagan role. Thirty years later, Harry Golden demonstrated that the Phagan case could still incite interest. His *A Little Girl is Dead* was one of the biggest sellers of 1965. But the latest chapter in the Mary Phagan story happened in the 1980s. In 1982 Alonzo Mann, an 83-year old resident of Bristol, Virginia, testified that Jim Conley killed Mary Phagan for $1.20. Mann said he was fourteen at the time of the crime and, nervous and frightened, did not tell all he knew at the trial. In his old age he was "making this statement because, finally, I want the record clear." At the time the State of Georgia refused to clear Frank of the crime, but in 1986, by which time Mann was dead, Georgia finally cleared Leo Frank of the murder of Mary Phagan.

The first version of "Little Mary Phagan" given here was collected by Mark Brantley Benge from Mrs. Artie Waggoner of Creston, Louisiana, in 1977. Mrs. Waggoner, who was Benge's aunt, kept this song and several other "song ballets" in a candy box. She got most of her songs from school friends and relatives. She recalled that a cousin living in Alabama gave her "Little Mary Fagan" (the way she spelled it) in 1925. Several aspects of the text suggest that this version was learned orally. It was, of course, Leo Frank, not Leo Benton, who was accused of murdering Phagan, and the murder occurred in Atlanta, Georgia. Newt Lee was the watchman, not Jim Newt, and the judge who presided over the case was named Roan, not Long. Finally, the spelling of Phagan's name as Fagan indicates that this text did not come from a printed source.

The second version comes from Mrs. Reba Cheyne of Fort Smith, Arkansas, and was sent to me on June 6, 1979. Mrs. Cheyne came from a singing family and learned the ballad from her father. Over the years she has forgotten large chunks of the song, the text given here being merely the words she still remembers.

Lord Barnie

COLLECTED BY PETER ROLLER, SEPTEMBER 1986, FROM LINDA BETH WALDRON,
WHITE SPRINGS, FLORIDA. TRANSCRIPTION BY DREW BEISSWENGER.

Lord Barnie was a brave hunting man,
And a-hunting he did ride.
With a gun all on his hunting arm,
And a broadsword by his side.

He rode till he came to his Aunt Jane's gate,
And ding dong he did ring.
And who was there but his own true love,
To rise up and bid him come in.

"Come in, come in, Lord Barnie," said she,
"And stay awhile with me.
I will give unto you a bright, shiny light,
And a seat beside of me."

"I can, I will, I must come in,
For I have but a moment to stay.
For the girl that I love much better than you
I must see 'fore breaking of day."

She took Lord Barnie all in her arms,
And her kisses were so sweet.
And she drew from his side a pin-pointed knife
And wounded Lord Barnie so deep.

It's three long hours till the breaking of day,
It's three long hours thought she.
Lord Barnie has died all in my arms
And it's time you've taken him away.

Some taken him by his golden curly locks,
Some taken him by his feet.
And threw Lord Barnie in Aunt Jane's well
Where the water was cold and deep.

This is a version of Child 68, "Young Hunting," a ballad most commonly encountered in the South. Nevertheless, it has been collected from traditional singers in Maine, Vermont, Missouri, Indiana, and Oklahoma as well as in Jamaica and Nova Scotia. It originated in Scotland and apparently passed directly to America without leaving much, if any, trace in Britain. Its earliest known publication was in 1776 but it certainly predates that year by several decades. The ballad exists in eight basic story types in America, of which the first is essentially that given in the present text. In most versions of this story type the narrative does not end with the disposal of the body in the well. Instead it concludes with a bird accusing the girl of the crime; she then attempts to bribe or threaten the animal but it reveals her guilt. A second story type is basically the same except that the motive for the killing is obliterated; the man refuses to spend the night because he wishes to see his parents. A third story type has the two main characters married. When the girl is walking in the garden she meets her father-in-law, who asks to see his son. The girl lies and says her husband is out hunting and is expected back soon, but the bird speaks up and reveals her deed. Men dig in the well and find the body; the girl is then hung. A fourth story type has the girl committing suicide on the night of her crime. In another story type the lord gives the girl's faithlessness as an excuse for leaving her; she chastises him for forsaking her, wishes she were dead, and regrets bearing him a child. In yet another type the murder occurs outside a barroom, the body is thrown in the well, and the girl announces to all what she has done. A seventh type consists mainly of a dialogue between the bird and the girl, in which the murder is briefly mentioned. The final story type tells the usual narrative up to the stabbing. The girl then begs him not to die, saying she has sent for doctors in the town who might be able to heal him. He asks her how he can live now that he is wounded and can feel his heart's blood dripping down to his feet? The episode of sending for doctors is thought to result from a misunderstanding of the Scottish "send for the king's duckers" episode. Duckers, men who searched the waters for the body, are entirely foreign to most Americans and thus were, so the theory goes, changed into the more comprehensible doctors.

Henry Belden thought that most American texts were traceable to a broadside version, although he could find no such text. The similarity of most recorded American texts seems to back up his opinion, but without further evidence his suggestion remains hypothetical. Most American texts are compressed and lack many of the details found in Child's versions, all of which were from Scotland. Such elements as the dressing up of the dead man and mounting him on his horse, the recovery of the body, and the intoxication of the protagonist before the murder, found in Child's texts, are missing from most American versions, including the one given here. In many of the reported American versions the talking bird episode is missing, a change that is in keeping with the American tendency to dispense with supernatural elements.

The present text was collected by Peter Roller in September 1986 from Linda Beth Waldron, White Springs, Florida. Mrs. Waldron is in her early forties and has lived in White Springs all her life. She learned her songs from her mother, Nancy Morgan, who grew up in Fargo, Georgia, a town close to the Florida border. Nancy, who learned her songs from family and friends, moved to White Springs shortly after her marriage and has lived there ever since. Neither Nancy nor Linda Beth has heard a version of "Lord Barnie" outside her family. Their text is fairly typical of American versions.

Lula Viers

COLLECTED MARCH 13, 1974, BY WILLIAM E. LIGHTFOOT FROM NORMA TURNER, DRIFT, KENTUCKY. TRANSCRIPTION BY W.K. MCNEIL.

Come all you young people
From all over the world,
And listen to this story
About a little girl.

Her name was Luly Viers,
In Auxier she did dwell,
In the state of old Kentucky,
A place we all know well.

Lula was persuaded
To leave her own dear home,
And to board the morning train
With John Colliers to roam.

They went to Elkhorn City,
Not many miles away;
They remained there at a hotel
Until the close of day.

But when the darkness fell,
They walked out as the style;
It was in cold December,
The wind was blowing wild.

While standing by the river,
Cold waters running deep,
John, he said to Luly,
"In the bottom you must sleep."

"Oh, do you mean it Johnny,
It surely can not be,
How could you bear to murder
Poor helpless girl like me?"

She threw her arms around him,
Before him she did kneel,
And around her neck he tied
A piece of railroad steel.

79

He threw her in the river,
Great bubbles gathered around,
They burst upon the water
With a sad and mournful sound.

John hastened to the depot,
He boarded the train for home,
A-thinking that his crime
Would never on earth be known.

But Luly was soon missing,
No place could she be found;
But in the Ohio River
Her body at last was found.

They took her from the river,
They carried her up to town,
And the piece of steel around her neck
Weighed even sixty pounds.

They sent for a reporter,
His name was Orydent,
He printed it in the paper
And around the world it went.

It went to Luly's mother,
While sitting in her home;
She quickly left her chair
To reach the telephone.

She called to headquarters,
She said, "I'll come and see
Oh, if it is my darling
Oh, surely it must be."

And when she reached the place,
Described the clothes she wore;
And when she saw the corpse,
She fainted to the floor.

John Colliers he was arrested,
Confined in the county jail;
But perhaps the electric chair
Should bear him on to hell.

This ballad deals with a crime that took place in October 1917. John
Coyer, a native of Auxier, a little mining community on the Big Sandy

River in Floyd County, Kentucky, courted Lula Viers shortly before joining the Army in World War I. When he returned on furlough he found out Lula was pregnant, a situation he evidently found undesirable. Somehow he persuaded the girl to take the local train to Elkhorn City, where he tied her up with a piece of steel and threw her weighted body in the Big Sandy River. Her body was not found until several months later, by which time it had washed a hundred miles downriver to a site near Ironton, Ohio. Coyer was caught and put in the Floyd County Jail. Before a trial occurred, Army authorities came and gained his release. Coyer went back into service and never came back to Floyd County. Thus, the hope expressed in the last line of the ballad never came to pass.

This version of "Lula Viers" was collected by William E. Lightfoot, March 13, 1974, from the singing of Norma Turner of Drift, Kentucky. Born in 1920, Mrs. Turner has always lived in Drift, which is located in Floyd County, the home county of Coyer and Viers. A folksinger with an extensive repertoire, Mrs. Turner learned many of her songs from her mother, including this version of "Lula Viers." Her mother lived about four miles from Auxier and possibly knew both Coyer and Viers.

Nellie Cropsey

COLLECTED BY LUCY MARIA COBB FROM MRS. BESSIE WESCOTT MIDGETT, MANTEO, NORTH CAROLINA, MAY 1927.

On the twentieth of November,
    A day we all remember well,
A handsome girl was coldly murdered,
    Of her story I will tell.

Girls, I pray you all take warning,
    Be careful how you trust a man,
For they will pretend they love you,
    Then will kill you if they can.

She had scarce passed sixteen summers,
    With eyes of blue and sunny curls,
Perfect were each handsome feature,
    With red lips shutting over pearls.

One night the lover called to see her,
    But they hardly spoke a word,
For they'd had a lover's quarrel,
    So the neighbors all had heard.

Three months later, her dear mother,
    Glimpsed a speck out on the river,
Oh 'tis my dear Nell I know,
    For my dream has told me so.

Soon they brought the body homeward,
    Oh how sad it was to see,
Father, mother, sisters, brothers,
    Round her bowed upon their knees.

Just behind them stood the lover,
    With his cold and hateful smile,
Making light of the dear parents,
    Weeping for the darling child.

We all think that Nell's an angel,
    Shining brightly as the stars,
As for Jim, the jealous lover
    Peeps behind prison bars.
Young man, I pray you to take warning
    Be careful what you do and say,
Remember life is very short,
    And there's a judgment day.

The book of life it will be brought,
    The Judge he will unfold,
And everything that you have done,
    Is there wrote down in gold.

The author of this ballad is identified in the following passage from Lucy Maria Cobb's M.A. thesis, *Traditional Ballads and Songs of Eastern North Carolina* (1927): "Some years ago a young girl disappeared from her home in Elizabeth City, in Pasquotank County; later her body was found in the river, and her sweetheart was tried and found guilty and sentenced to the penitentiary. There sprang up a song about the occurrence, sung all over the state and people did not know the author. In Manteo, May, 1927, I met the author, Mrs. Bessie Wescott Midgett, who wrote it for me, along with a number of others of her own composition. She did not know that it had ever appeared in the state papers. It had been printed without the name of the author." Elsewhere Cobb speaks of Mrs. Midgett as "a pleasant, attractive, middle-aged woman, who must have been a young girl in her teens when she wrote the song about twenty-two years ago." If Cobb is correct, this means the song was written about 1905, i.e., about three or four years after the events that occasioned it.

In hopes of following up on Mrs. Midgett's story, letters were sent to newspapers and historical societies in the Manteo area but no answers have been forthcoming. Most likely she is long deceased, for sixty years ago she was middle-aged. According to Cobb, she wrote numerous songs on local events that she then set to old tunes. Unfortunately, Cobb doesn't include the melody she used for "Nellie Cropsey" or indicate elsewhere what melody was used. In volume IV of the *Frank C. Brown Collection of North Carolina Folklore* (Durham, North Carolina: Duke University Press, 1957), p. 327, there is a melody line for one text of "Nellie Cropsey" that bears a strong resemblance to "The Lexington Miller," so that is probably the tune Midgett utilized. If so, it was a good choice because the melody is well known in the southern United States.

What was the event that occasioned the ballad? It was one of the most sensational murder cases in turn-of-the-century eastern North Carolina. In 1901 Nellie (Ella Maude) Cropsey, the daughter of an Elizabeth City farmer, was murdered. Her sweetheart Jim Wilcox, a shipyard worker and son of a former sheriff, was the prime suspect. In early November 1901 he and Nellie had a lover's quarrel and for two weeks Wilcox stayed away from Cropsey's home. Then, on the evening of the twentieth he came to her house and talked to the nineteen-year-old girl and her family. Just before leaving shortly after eleven o'clock,

Wilcox asked to see Nellie in the hall for a minute. Her family never saw her alive again. On December 27 her body was found in the Pasquotank River, about 150 yards in front of her home. Wilcox was arrested and, largely because of his cold, impassive attitude throughout the investigation, public feeling against him ran high. It was so strong, in fact, that the local naval reserve was called out to guard him. In March 1902 he was convicted of murder and sentenced to be hanged but on appeal he was granted a new trial. In March 1903 he was again convicted, but this time he was sentenced to thirty years in the state penitentiary. He was pardoned on December 20, 1918, and on December 4, 1934, almost sixteen years to the day of his pardon, he committed suicide.

At least six different ballads were written about Nellie Cropsey, but only the present ballad and one set to the tune of "The Jealous Lover" achieved any lasting popularity. Of these two, Mrs. Midgett's ballad seems to be the one that has enjoyed the more widespread and longer-lived popularity. Cobb and other collectors have found sufficient evidence to refute G. Malcolm Laws's claim [*Native American Balladry* (Philadelphia: The American Folklore Society, 1964), p. 269] that it is of doubtful currency in tradition. Given above is the text written for Cobb by Mrs. Midgett. Note that although the ballad is factually correct in most instances it incorrectly states that it was three months before Cropsey's body was found. In Anglo-American culture the number three is magical, so the ballad may have been molded to conform with the expectations of its intended audience. In other words, art took precedence here over the goal of factual journalistic reporting.

Pearl Bryan

COLLECTED IN 1977 BY BURT FEINTUCH FROM GLADYS PACE, SUMMER SHADE,
KENTUCKY. TRANSCRIPTION BY DREW BEISSWENGER.

Deep, deep down in the valley,
Where the flowers bloom and fade,
There lies our own Pearl Bryan
In a cold and silent grave.

She died not broken hearted,
Nor by disease she fell,
But in one moment parted
From those she loved so well.

One evening when the moon shone brightly,
And the stars were shining too,
Into her lighted cottage
Her jealous lover drew.

Saying, "Pearl, let's take a ramble
Into the woods and meadows gay,
Where no one can disturb us,
We'll name our wedding day."

The night was cold and dreary,
She was afraid to stay.
Of wandering she grew weary,
And would have retraced her way.

"Retrace your way, no never.
These woods you'll roam no more.
Long, long they'll wait your coming
At your own little cottage door.

No arms can take you from me,
Nor from me can you fly.
No earthly soul can hear you;
You instantly must die."

Down on her knees before him,
She pleaded for her life.
Into her snow white bosom,
He plunged his fatal knife.

"Oh, what have I done, Scott Jackson,
That you should take my life?
You know I've always loved you
And would have been your wife."

The birds sing in the morning,
And mournful were their tunes.
They found Pearl Bryan lying
In a cold and silent tomb.

She died away from home and friends,
Out in that lonely spot.
Take heed, take heed, believe this, girls.
Don't let this be your lot.

On February 1, 1896, a young boy discovered the headless body of a young woman half buried in leaves and brush in a farmer's field near Fort Thomas, Kentucky. The following day a coroner revealed that the victim was five months pregnant; immediately it was assumed that the father of the baby was the girl's murderer. Until the body was identified that possibility was of little help, but then, on February 5, the victim's identity became known. She was Pearl Bryan, twenty-three-year-old daughter of a prosperous farmer in Greencastle, Indiana. The following day one of her boyfriends, Scott Jackson, a Cincinnati dental student, was arrested for murder. A few days later Jackson's roommate, Alonzo Walling, was arrested on the same charge. In the subsequent trial the prosecution argued that Jackson and Walling had attempted to perform an abortion on Pearl and when this failed they decapitated her. The two men were convicted and hanged on the same gallows March 20, 1897. To the last they protested their innocence, blaming a friend of theirs named William Wood. Bryan's head was never found.

At least five different ballads about the Bryan case were written and four of them entered folk tradition. One of these was a reworking of an older piece generally known as "The Jealous Lover," a fact that has occasionally led some ballad students to confuse all Pearl Bryan songs with the older number. All of the Bryan ballads employ stereotypes common to formulaic ballad traditions about murdered girls. For example, the fact that Pearl was beheaded is suppressed in most of the ballads because it is not among the methods by which girls traditionally meet their end in murdered-girl songs. In the ballads Pearl is pictured as innocent, trusting, and helpless against the lover-murderer and listeners are reminded that she has a family to grieve after her. Jackson, on the other hand, is depicted as clever and brutal and rarely has a family to grieve after him. Several of the ballads employ the plea followed by refusal. Pearl's sister, occasionally with another family member, unsuccessfully begs the murderer to reveal the whereabouts of her sister's head. Some of these "facts" do not agree with the realities of the case even though they are mainly in agreement with journalistic accounts of the day.

Various Pearl Bryan ballads have been collected from folk tradition in Indiana, Utah, North Carolina, West Virginia, Florida, Illinois, Ohio, Georgia, and Kentucky. Except for an occasional version titled "The Jealous Lover" all of the ballads are named "Pearl Bryan." The present version belongs to the cycle G. Malcolm Laws calls Pearl Bryan I, i.e., a member of the "Jealous Lover" group. It was collected in 1977 by Burt Feintuch from Gladys Pace, Summer Shade, Kentucky. Born in 1916 in Nobob, Kentucky, Pace learned most of her songs from her mother but picked up some from magazines. She sings primarily while working and driving or at religious singing conventions. At the time this ballad was collected she and her husband were running a dairy farm. They have since moved but still live in the same area. She probably learned "Pearl Bryan" from her mother.

La Hija Desobediente
(The Disobedient Daughter)

COLLECTED BY MARY V. MELLEN FROM JOSÉ RICARDO ARMENDARIZ, EL PASO, TEXAS, DECEMBER 6, 1967.

Año de mil nueve cientos,
Presente lo tengo yo.
En el barrio de Saltillo,
Rosita Alvidrez murio.

Su mama se lo decia,
"Hija, no vayas al baile,"
"Mama no tengo la cupla
Que a mi me gustan los bailes."

Su mama se lo decia,
Su padre con mas razon,
"Hija, querida de mi alma,
Cuidate de una traicion."

Hipolito llego al baile,
Y a se dirigia.
Como era la mas bonita,
Rosita, lo desairo.

"Rosita no me desaires,
La gente lo va a notar."
"Pues que digan lo que quieran,
Contigo no he de bailar."

Hecho mano a la cintura.
Y una pistola saco,
Ya la pobre de Rosita,
Nomas tres tiros le dio.

Ya Rosita esta en el cielo,
Dondole cuenta al Criador,
Y hipolito esta en la carcel,
Donde su declaracion.

The year of 1900
Is present in my mind.
In the neighborhood of Saltillo,
Rosita Alvidrez died.

Her mother told her,
"Daughter, do not go to the dance."
"Mother, it's not my fault
If I like dances."

Her mother told her,
Her father with more of a reason also told her
"Beloved daughter of my soul,
Watch out for foul play."

Hipolito arrived at the dance,
And went to Rosita.
Since she was the prettiest one,
Rosita snubbed him.

"Rosita, don't snub me.
People are going to notice."
"Well, let them say what they want,
I won't dance with you."

His hand went to his waist,
And he took out a gun,
And he shot poor Rosita three times.

Rosita is now in Heaven,
Giving an account to the Creator
And Hipolito is in jail,
Giving his confession.

Although there is a traditional *corrido* named "El Hijo Desobediente" (The Disobedient Son) and a very popular Hispanic legend known as "La Hija Desobediente" (The Disobedient Daughter) or "The Devil at the Dance," this *corrido* is different from either one. It bears closest resemblance to the legend in that the girl attends the dance against her parent's wishes, although, of course, the man she meets is human, not the Devil. That the girl meets with foul play is almost a foregone conclusion, and perhaps her stern fate which results from disobeying parental orders and the similarity of the story to the legend accounts for the widespread popularity of this seemingly undistinguished tale. Versions of the song have been collected in New Mexico, Texas, Arizona, and California and may be even more widely known than this list suggests. The usual title is "Rosita Alvirez"; the name Alvidrez seems to be peculiar to the version given here. The present text was collected December 6, 1967, by Mary V. Mellen from José Ricardo Armendariz, El Paso, Texas. Armendariz was born in 1935 and learned his songs from his grandparents, natives of Mexico who moved to Texas.

Ballads of Tragedies and Disasters

The Cloudburst

COLLECTED BY MERCEDES STEELY FROM MRS. NORA JOHNSON, EBENEZER, NORTH CAROLINA, APRIL 1935. TRANSCRIPTION BY MERCEDES STEELY AND JAN PHILIP SCHINHAN.

In the month of July and the year of sixteen,
The worst tropical storm that ever was seen
Made its way from the ocean wide
And struck with force on the mountain-side.

At the head of Jack Branch there was children five,
A mother and father and all alive;
They stood in the door and the rain came down;
They saw how quickly it covered the ground.

The pleading words of little Perry was heard:
"Together to the pines let us go," he said;
But the words of the boy had scarcely been spoken,
When the windows of Heaven was thrown wide open.

The down-pour came with a 'riffic ro',
It struck the house; they were thrown to the flo'.
A new-born babe in a cradle at rest
The mother snatched up and pressed to her breast.

The house went down, it struck a tree,
They were all thrown out except the three;
The house went down and the horses, too,
And the neighbor says, "There are work to do!"

Julius and Wilson made their way
To the dear old place that awful day,
But when they got there, no house was found;
They had to take to higher ground.

Down in an old house which Wilson built,
There Lolas and Lily and the children knelt;
Said he to Lolas and Lily, too,
"Are your children all saved? I only see two!"

"Oh no," says he, "I fear they have drowned;
They haven't been seen since the house went down."
Down in a bottom by the Sinclair Pond
The bodies of Lolas and Johnnie was found.

But poor little Perry has never been found,
He sleeps somewhere beneath the ground,
With a bed of mud and a piller of clay;
He may not be found till the last great Day,
When angels come and the trumpet sounds
To wake the dead that's under the ground.

O Thou dear Lord, wilt Thou, dear Love,
Prepare them all to meet Thee above,
That they may praise Thee face to face,
And sing with Thee (a loving) (redeeming) grace.*

This seems to be a purely North Carolina ballad, more specifically a Wake County song. The informant, Mrs. Nora Johnson, explained the song's origin in the following way: "This happened fifteen years ago [i.e., in 1920]. I know the man that helped find the children—Dave Baumgartner. He never ate no more meat in six months. The dogs found one of 'em's feet stickin' out of the mud . . . Him and his uncle made this song themselves . . . It happened in the mountains near Lenoir County, Lolas and Lily were the husband and wife. Jenny, Louis, and Perry were killed."

The collector, Mercedes Steely, remarks that the "tune suits the words and the general mood of the piece very well indeed." She also adds that the melody resembles that of a version of "Death Is a Melancholy Call" that she recorded from another singer in Mrs. Johnson's community. Even so, this is not the tune generally associated with that religious song. Ebenezer, North Carolina, Mrs. Johnson's home town, was eleven miles northwest of Raleigh, the state capital, but has since been swallowed up by the city.

Other than the name, Steely provides little information about Mrs. Johnson. This ballad was collected in April 1935, during which time Steely was collecting material for her M.A. thesis *The Folk-Songs of Ebenezer Community* (1936), which was written for the English Department at the University of North Carolina, Chapel Hill. Judging from the number of items she contributed, Johnson was one of Steely's major informants.

---

*Concerning these alternatives it was explained by the informant that "ary one of 'em will do."

The Romish Lady

COLLECTED BY THEODORE GARRISON FROM MRS. MARTHA GARRISON, MARSHALL,
ARKANSAS, JULY 1942. TRANSCRIBED BY THEODORE GARRISON.

There was a Romish lady
Brought up in popery;
Her mother always taught her
The priest she must obey.
Oh pardon me, dear Mother,
I humble pray thee now,
For unto these false idols
I can no longer bow.

Assisted by her handmaid
A Bible she concealed,
And there obtained instructions
Till God His love revealed.
No more she prostrated herself,
And pictures decked with gold;
But soon she was betrayed,
And her Bible from her stoled.

I'll bow to my dear Jesus;
I'll worship God unseen;
I'll live by faith forever.
The works of men are vain.
I can not worship angels,
Nor pictures made by men.
Dear Mother, use your pleasure,
But pardon if you can.

With grief and great vexation
Her mother straight did go
To inform the Romish clergy
The cause of all her woe.
The priests were soon assembled
And for the maid did call,
And forced her in the dungeon
To affright her soul withal.

The more they strove to affright her,
The more she did endure;
Although her age was tender,
Her faith was strong and sure.
The chains of gold so costly
They from this lady took;
And she, with all her spirit,
The pride of life forsook.

Before the pope they brought her
In hopes of her return,
And there she was condemned
In horrid flames to burn.
Before the place of torment
They brought her speedily;
With lifted hands to heaven
She then agreed to die.

There being many ladies
Assembled at the place,
She raised her eyes to heaven
And begged supplying grace.
Weep not, you tender ladies;
Shed not a tear for me.
While my poor body's burning,
My soul the Lord will see.

Yourselves you need to pity
On Zion's deep decay.
Dear ladies, turn to Jesus;
No longer make delay.
In came her raving mother
Her daughter to behold,
And in her hand she brought her
Some pictures decked with gold.

Oh take from me those idols;
Remove them from my sight.
Restore to me my Bible
In which I take delight.
Alas, my aged mother,
Why on my ruin bent?
'Twas you that did betray me,
But I am innocent.

Tormentors, use your pleasure,
And do as you think best;
I hope my blessed Jesus
Will take my soul to rest.
Soon as these words were spoken,
Up stepped the man of death,
And kindled up the fire
To stop her mortal breath.

Instead of golden bracelets,
With chains they bound her fast.
She cried, "My God, give power;
Now must I die at last.
With Jesus and His angels
Forever I shall dwell.
God, pardon priests and people;
And so I bid farewell."

This is an American version of the ballad "The Lady's Daughter of Paris" that is sung by Merrythought in John Fletcher and Francis Beaumont's *The Knight of the Burning Pestle* (1611). Here the "lady's daughter, of Paris properly" has been replaced by a "Romish lady." A later version is given in the *Roxburghe Ballads* under the wordy title "A Rare Example of a Vertuous Maid in Paris, who was by her own Mother procured to be put in Prison, thinking thereby to compel her to Popery; but she continued to the end and finished her life in the fire." Despite its English origin it is virtually unknown there today but is fairly well known in America, its survival aided by several broadside and songbook printings. For example, the ballad appeared in the *Hesperian Harp* (1848) and in an 1854 reprint of William Walker's *The Southern Harmony*. That the ballad was very popular can be seen from its several parodies, at least one of which entered folk tradition for a time. According to William Henry Herndon, Abraham Lincoln's law partner and biographer, when the future president was a boy in Indiana he considered "The Romish Lady" one of his favorite songs.

"The Romish Lady" or "Death of a Romish Lady" (the other title by which it is commonly known) has been collected from traditional singers in Ohio, Alabama, Kentucky, North Carolina, Missouri, Indiana, Michigan, Mississippi, Florida, Texas, Virginia, and Illinois. There is little variation in titles or lyrics, suggesting the possibility that print has played a stronger role in its preservation than at first seems the case. The present text was collected July 1942 by Theodore R. Garrison from his step-grandmother Mrs. Martin Garrison, Marshall, Arkansas. Mrs. Garrison (1863–1944) was born in Searcy County (where Marshall is located) but spent part of her childhood in Missouri, where her father was forced to go because of his pro-Union sentiments during the Civil War. Garrison thinks that she may have learned "The Romish Lady" from the 1854 reprint of *The Southern Harmony*, but because the two melodies are not identical that seems unlikely.

Schaladi

COLLECTED BY GEORGE CONWAY, APRIL 1965, FROM MRS. LULA JAYNE HARTSELL, WASHINGTON COUNTY, TENNESSEE. TRANSCRIPTION BY ANNETTE WOLFORD.

Young Schaladi lived on a mountain side,
A wild and a lonely side;
No building was for many miles around
Except her father's cot.

Her father loved to see her dressed
Just as fine as a city belle,
But she was the only girl that he had,
And he loved his daughter well.

The evening sun was bending low
When a well-known voice she heard,
And o'er the mount to the little cottage door
Young Charlie's sleigh did appear.

'Tis a village fifteen miles away,
'Tis a merry ball tonight;
The air is cold and chilling as death,
But her heart was warm and bright.

"Oh no, oh no," her father said,
" 'Tis a dreadful night you know;
The air is cold and chilling as death,
And you'll catch your death of cold."

"Oh no, oh no," the daughter said,
"My blanket's lined too well;
Besides I have my fine silken shawl
To wrap my neck all about."

Her shawl and bonnet she put on,
Then stepped into the sleigh,
And o'er the ice and snow they went
And o'er the hills far away.

Young Charlie he drove up to the ballroom door
And quickly he jumped out.
"How sit you now like a monument?
You have no power to stir."

He asked her once, he asked her thrice,
But still she did not stir;
He asked her for her hands again,
And she never said a word.

He bore the corpse into the sleigh
As quickly he hurried home;
And darting up to the little cottage door,
Oh how her parents did mourn.

They mourned the loss of their dear child,
And Charlie he mourned too,
Until they both did die of grief
And they both buried in one tomb.

This is a unique title for this ballad which is usually known as "Young Charlotte" or "Fair Charlotte," and probably results from a misunderstanding of the word "Charlotte." The only other name by which it is widely known is "The Frozen Girl." There has been much discussion about the authorship of this ballad, which at one time was thought to be the work of William Lorenzo Carter, a blind poet and ballad-singer from Bensontown, Vermont. Carter supposedly wrote the song sometime prior to 1833 and hawked copies of it in his travels across New England and New York State. According to another claim the song was written shortly after the death of a Charlotte Dills, who was frozen to death at Auburn, Indiana, in 1862. Most authorities, however, now agree that it was the work of Seba Smith (1792–1868), a Maine native generally known for his humorous writings such as *The Life and Writings of Major Jack Downing* (1833) and *My Thirty Years Out of the Senate* (1859).

Smith read a story published in 1831 about a Charlotte J— who was found dead in her "bower," all dressed for a ball. That was the source for the heroine's name but the incident that inspired the song was a story that appeared in the February 8, 1840, issue of the *New York Observer.* Titled "A Corpse Going to a Ball," the article concerned an unnamed young lady who froze to death on January 1, 1840, while on her way to a dance. Smith's ballad, also titled "A Corpse Going to a Ball," appeared in the December 28, 1843, issue of *The Rover.* From there it went on to widespread popularity; it has been collected in Vermont, Missouri, Illinois, Indiana, North Carolina, Colorado, Michigan, Arkansas, Utah, Virginia, Florida, Tennessee, Texas, New York, Iowa, California, New Jersey,

Wisconsin, Kentucky, Ohio, Pennsylvania, Nebraska, West Virginia, Maine, and Newfoundland.

Names of the principal characters rarely vary; the girl's name is Charlotte and the boy's name is Charlie. The present text is, of course, an exception to this general rule. Considering the song's popularity and its very serious nature it is surprising that it has rarely been parodied. One such parody, "Git Up off'n the Floor, Hannah! (or A Bitter New Year's Eve)," was written and recorded by Red Ingle and the Natural Seven in the late 1940s, but it has made no inroads on the folk tradition.

The present version was collected April 1965 by George Conway from Mrs. Lula Jayne Hartsell, Washington County, Tennessee. Unfortunately, no other information is available about either the collector or informant.

Three Perished in the Snow

COLLECTED BY BYRON ARNOLD FROM REV. LYTLE BURNS, FLORENCE, ALABAMA, JUNE 9, 1947. TRANSCRIPTION BY BYRON ARNOLD.

'Twas on a dreadful stormy night,
The snow was falling fast,
A woman and three little babes,
Were traveling through the blast.

While traveling thru the cold, cold snow,
These little ones would cry,
"Oh, Mamma, Mamma, make us warm,
Oh, Mamma we will die."*

Next morning when the sun came out
The snow was melting fast;
Three darlings lay side by side
In one fond loving clasp.

The farmer heard the sad, sad news;
It made him weep to know
That on the dreadful stormy night
Three perished in the snow.

Toll, toll the village bells;
Let all good people know
That on one dreadful stormy night
Three perished in the snow.*

Despite Catskill folksinger George Edwards's claim that his mother wrote this ballad after the famous blizzard of 1888, it is actually a product of the nineteenth-century music hall. Both words and music were written by Eddie C. Fox and the song was introduced in 1878 by Fred Waltz of Sweatnam's Minstrels. The ballad also appeared in songbooks of the 1880s and 1890s. Fox was a mildly successful songwriter of the day with several other compositions to his credit. The most important of

---

*The second ending of the music should be used for this verse.

these are "Nell the Little Belle" and "She's Lovely as a Rose" (both 1867). In addition, Fox did a popular arrangement of "Goodbye, Liza Jane" (c. 1880).

To date "Three Perished in the Snow" has been reported from traditional singers in Alabama, New York, and Virginia. It is also known as "She Perished in the Snow," the original title. There is great variation in the lyrics of the reported versions. The Alabama text given here seems somewhat incomplete, although as far as the singer was concerned nothing is missing. But the listener never learns what happened to the mother, a problem that is resolved in the New York version. In that set of lyrics there are only "two darling babes," so the mother is the third one who perishes. The New York text also has an extra verse explaining in some detail what happened just before the three died.

The present version was collected June 9, 1947, by Byron Arnold from the Reverend Lytle Burns, Florence, Alabama. Mr. Burns was a Primitive Baptist preacher who was very proud of his fifty-one years of service to the church. He learned "Three Perished in the Snow" in 1885 "from an old traveling man selling musical instruments." He accompanied his own singing by playing a fiddle in a cross tuning (i.e., tuned to a chord rather than standard tuning) with the two lower strings functioning as a drone bass, while the melody notes were played on the upper two strings. Burns also played a one-string dulcimer which he sometimes used to accompany his "fasola" singing. He was the author of a book of poems. For more information on Arnold see the notes to "Billy Grimes."

The Titanic

COLLECTED APRIL 3, 1951, BY IRENE J. CARLISLE FROM EARVEN ANGLIN, SPRINGDALE, ARKANSAS. TRANSCRIPTION BY DOROTHY OSWALD.

On the seventeenth day of April,*
Nineteen hundred and twelve,
The ship by the name of *Titanic*
From Liverpool left, with the swells.
It was headed for New York City
With the cargoes of wealth and toll;
On the shores of Newfoundland Island
She sank in the waters so cold.

CHORUS:

As the mighty ship was sinking
In the cold and icy sea,
The last that the bands was heard to play
Was "Nearer, My God, to thee."

On board of the mighty vessel
Men with millions did ride;
The doctor, the lawyer, the merchant,
The rich, the poor, with their bride.
The gambler with all of his money;
The trimes went down the same;
The sheeler now died with the cunning;
The slayer now died with the slain.

CHORUS: (same as before)

---

*The *Titanic* sank on April 15, 1912, not April 17.

The Titantic

COLLECTED MAY 10, 1951, BY IRENE J. CARLISLE FROM LULA DAVIS, FAYETTEVILLE,
ARKANSAS. TRANSCRIPTION BY DOROTHY OSWALD.

Sailing out on the *Titantic*,
Some ninety miles from shore,
When suddenly it struck an iceberg,
And sank to rise no more.

CHORUS:

Lost on the great *Titantic*,
Sinking to rise no more;
The number, sixteen hundred
That failed to reach the shore

There were paupers, merchants, and rich men
Sailing out on this boat;
And when it sank in the ocean
You could see their bodies float.

The men stood back like heroes,
Sending their wives to the shore;
They kissed, shook hands, and parted,
To meet on earth no more.

The band was playing sadly,
"Nearer, My God, To Thee;"
It seemed to play its utmost
As it sank in the deep blue sea.

The Titanic

COLLECTED JUNE 21, 1951, BY GEORGE W. BOSWELL FROM MRS. JAMES K. NASH OF HICKMAN COUNTY, TENNESSEE. TRANSCRIPTION BY GEORGE W. BOSWELL.

As the moon rose in glory,
Drifting to the golden west,
She told her sad, sad story:
Sixteen hundred have gone to rest.

The watchman was lying down dreaming,
Yes, dreaming a sad, sad dream;
He dreamed the *Titanic* was sinking
Far out on the deep blue sea.

He woke and called the rich man,
Told him to come to life;
Told him to save his baby
And also his darling wife.

The rich man, he must have been drinking.
Knowing that he had done wrong,
He tried to win the record
And let the *Titanic* go down.

When he spied the *Titanic* was sinking
They fell down upon their knees
And cried, "Oh, Lord, have mercy!
And what will become of me?"

The band was out there playing,
Yes, playing out on the sea.
When they spied the *Titanic* was sinking
Played "Nearer, My God to Thee."

105

When the sad news reached the landing
That the *Titanic* had gone down,
Many a poor widow and orphan
Was walking all over the town.

The little children were crying
"Oh, Mama has gone to stay."
But surely they will invent something
That will weigh the *Titanic* some day.

On Sunday, April 14, 1912, the Royal Mail Steamer *Titanic,* at the time the largest ship afloat, was on its maiden voyage from Liverpool to New York. The crew and 2,224 passengers were aboard and, when the ship struck an iceberg at full speed, 1,513 lives were lost as the steamer went to the bottom of the Atlantic. This great loss of life was in large part attributable to a lack of preparation; that is, the ship simply did not have enough lifeboats to accommodate the number of passengers on board. The tragedy made headlines around the world and was promptly commemorated in several songs, at least five of which had some life in folk tradition. Perhaps the most popular of these is the C version given here, a ballad that is taken seriously by some people and as a comic song by others.

Ballads about the sinking of the *Titanic* generally borrowed their melodies from previously existing songs. Newman I. White thought all of them could be traced to a folksong about the wreck of an early Mississippi River steamboat. The B text here takes its melody from "Lost on the Lady Elgin," a popular song of 1860 by Henry Clay Work (1832–1884). The C text takes its tune from a religious song titled "Dulcimer" written by Freeman Lewis (1780–1859). All of these songs reaffirm the powers of the Almighty or proclaim the futility of earthly grandeur and riches. Songs and toasts (narrative poems, frequently epical, involving an extended battle between protagonists) in Afro-American folk tradition use the tragedy for the same purposes but also add some others. Whites are excoriated for excluding blacks from the vessel, and in toasts about Shine, a fictional black stoker aboard the *Titanic,* a legendary confrontation between a black worker and the white world occurs. In this encounter Shine emerges victorious.

The first two *Titanic* texts given here were collected by Irene J. Carlisle. Text number one is from Earven Anglin of Springdale, Arkansas, and was recorded April 3, 1951. A native of Cave Springs, Arkansas, Anglin was about thirty-five years old at the time of collection. He was co-owner of a Springdale garage where he worked as a mechanic. Anglin did not recall where he learned the song but insisted that the apparently meaningless words in the second stanza are given exactly as he heard

106

them. The second text was recorded from the singing of Lula Davis in Fayetteville, Arkansas, May 10, 1951. Mrs. Davis was born at Iconium, Missouri, but her family moved to Ozark, Arkansas, when she was only seven years old. She and her husband moved to Fayetteville in 1927 and lived there or in nearby Springdale, Arkansas, afterwards. Mrs. Davis was a member of a family that had great regard for old ballads and folksongs. A small, frail woman who worked in a local garment factory, Davis reportedly had a sweet tremulous singing voice. She learned this version of "The Great *Titanic*" as a girl in Missouri, so she had, at the time of collection, known it for more than thirty-five years. The third text was collected June 21, 1951, by George W. Boswell from the singing of Mrs. James K. Nash of Hickman County, Tennessee. She probably learned the ballad from the singing of her mother, Ollie Palestine Smith Stevens, who was born in 1873.

The third text is a version of the only Titanic ballad that can be traced to a specific songwriter; it was written several years after the tragedy by a native of Searcy County, Arkansas. Seth Newton Mize (1901– 1977), began playing the fiddle and guitar at age fifteen and performed on both instruments for the rest of his life. He was especially well-known for his old-time fiddle playing which he accompanied with a fast jig step. Mize also tried his hand at writing songs, and although his output wasn't prolific he succeeded in accomplishing something few persons live to see. That is, he wrote songs that actually entered oral tradition and became folksongs during his lifetime. One of these was called "After the Sinking of the *Titanic* or just "The *Titanic*" and was recorded on a number of occasions by country artists such as Tom Darby and Jimmie Tarlton (although that version was not released until several years after its recording) and the Carter Family. None of these recordings was what could be called a big hit but they undoubtedly helped spread the ballad.

Just when Mize wrote his Titanic ballad is uncertain but it seems unlikely that it was composed prior to 1916 when he started playing music. Possibly it was as late as the early 1920s, but whatever the date it is certain that the song got into oral tradition and away from Mize. This is attested to both by the various commercial recordings, all of which vary from each other lyrically, and by the failure of the record companies to list Mize as the song's creator. There is, of course, the possibility that lack of acknowledgment was merely to avoid paying royalties, but, since record companies were usually quite good about checking out ownership of copyrights, it seems more likely that the performers simply didn't know who had written the ballad.

The Vulture

AS SUNG BY DEE HICKS, TINCHTOWN, TENNESSEE, AT THE FIFTIETH ANNIVERSARY OF THE ARCHIVE OF FOLK SONG, WASHINGTON, D.C., IN 1978. TRANSCRIPTION BY DREW BEISSWENGER.

I've been among those mighty Alps,
I've wandered through their vales.
I've heard the oldest mountaineer
Relate their dismal tales.
But when around financher cottage homes,
But when their daily work were o'er,
They would talk of those who had disappeared
And ne'er returned no more.

It's there I from a shepherd learned
The dangerous part of fear.
He told a mortal story there
That mothers might not hear.
Oh, the tears were standing in his eyes,
Oh, his voice so low it bust.
Though wiping all those tears away
He told his story thus:

"Among the mighty and craggy rocks
The rapture vulture dwells.
He never fattens on the prey
Till he can from afar it smells.
Though it's patient waiting hours and hours
Upon some lonely rock,
Oh, then choosing out his true lamb,
His victim from some flock.

108

"It was on one clear September morn,
The sun was rolling high,
When from my children on the green
I heard a dismal cry.
As if some awful deed were done,
Oh, they cried deep in vain.
Oh, a cry I humbly trust to God
I ne'er may hear again.

"I hurried out to learn the cause
Though all hellum with fright.
My infants never ceased to scream
When to their friend lost sight.
Oh, I missed the youngest of my babes,
Oh, the darling of my care.
Oh, when something caught my searching eye,
Slow-sailing through the air.

"Now what a hard spectacle
To meet a father's eye.
My infant to be a vulture's prey,
Just hasten'd o'er to die.
But, then off to many a shed,
And off to many a cave.
No human creature could now prevent
This infant child to save.

"My infant reached his little hands
Imploring unto me,
While struggling with the rapture bird
So vainly to get free.
And at intervals I heard him cry,
Oh, so loud he shrieked and screamed,
Until upon that azure sky
A glistening spot he seemed.

"The vulture flopped his sail-like wings
Though heavily he flew.
Until upon that sun's broad face
He seemed into my view.
But, oh, once I thought I saw him stoop,
Oh, that infant for to lie.
It was all but an illusion 'fore
For all that vantage 'quired. (Uncertain, this is what Dee seems to
    be singing.)

109

"One year went by, then rolling times,
This child was ne'er forgot.
Until a daring hunter climbed
Up to a lofty spot.
When there upon that crowded old rock
Where the climbers ne'er had reached,
Oh, there lay the bones of an infant one
The elements had bleached.

"I hurried up those craggy rocks,
I could not stay away.
I knew that was my infant's bones
Just hastening to decay.
But the tattered garment it still remained
Though torn to many a thread.
Oh, the crimson cap that he wore that morn
Was still upon his head."

The Vulture of the Alps

FROM MRS. ATTIE HART DILLINGHAM, PLANO, TEXAS, AUGUST 21, 1985.

I've lived among the mighty Alps,
I've wandered through their vales,
And heard the honest mountaineer
Relate their dismal tales.
While sitting 'round a blazing hearth
My daily task was o'er;
They spoke of those who disappeared
And ne'er was heard of more.

And there I from a shepherd learned
A narrative of fear.
A tale to rend a mortal's heart
Which mothers might not hear.
The tears were standing in his eyes,
His voice was tremulous,
Though wiping all his tears away
He told his story thus:

"It is among the mighty Alps
The ravenous vulture dwells.
Who fatten not upon the prey
That from afar he smells.
But patient waiting day by day
Upon a lofty rock,
He settle down to over-power
The victim from the flock.

"One cloudless Sabbath summer morn,
The sun was rising high,
When from my children on the green
There rose a fearful cry.
As if some awful deed was done,
They shrieked aloud in vain.
Such cries I humbly trust to God
I ne'er shall hear again.

"I rushing out to learn the cause
Though overwhelmed with fright.
My children never ceased to shriek
To see their friend in sight.
I missed the youngest of my babes,
The darling of my care,
When something caught my searching eye,
Slow-sailing through the air.

111

"The vulture flapped his sail-like wings
Though heavily he flew.
A mote upon the sun's broad face
He seemed unto my view.
My little infant stretched his arms
Imploringly to me
And struggled with the ravenous bird
All vainly to get free.

"At intervals we heard his cry,
Though loud he shrieked and screamed,
A mote upon the azure sky,
A glistening spot he seemed.

"All search was made, and years had passed,
The child was never got
Until a daring hunter climbed
Upon that lofty spot.
He clambered up that ragged cliff
Where shoe had never reached.
He spied an infant's fleshless bones
The elements had bleached.

"I struggled up that rugged cliff,
I could not stay away.
I knew they were my infant's bones
A-hastening to decay.
A tattered garment still remained
Though torn to many a shred.
The crimson cap he wore that morn
Was yet upon his head."

This was the first published song by the Hutchinson Family, one of the most popular singing groups in America during the 1840s and 1850s. The group was made up from the thirteen children of Jesse and Mary Hutchinson of Milford, New Hampshire. They became so successful that a town, Hutchinson, Minnesota, was named after them. Although the group performed primarily in the Northeast they were strong advocates of many issues of national importance in their day, lending their support to such causes as temperance, the abolition of slavery, and the suffrage movement. Their most popular song was "The Old Granite State," a tribute to their native New Hampshire, but they also introduced or popularized "The Cot Where We Were Born," "Excelsior," "Go Call the Doctor and Be Quick, or Anti-Calomel," "Hannah's at the Window Binding Shoes," "If I Were a Voice," "The Grave of Bonaparte," "The

Snowstorm," "The Song of the Shirt," "Ship on Fire," "The Maniac," and "Uncle Sam's Farm," among others.

"The Vulture of the Alps" was a poem that Judson Hutchinson (1817–1859) found in *The First Class Reader* and set to music. Luke Newland, an Albany, New York, fan who had a music store, published the ballad in 1842 with a lithograph on the cover of a vulture grasping a child in its talons. Both texts of the song given here are derived from the Hutchinson original, although they do contain an additional verse (the second one), also of literary origin. These are the only known examples of this ballad from oral tradition. The first text is from Dee Hicks of Tinchtown, Tennessee; it is given as he sang it in 1978 at the Fiftieth Anniversary of the Archive of Folk Song in Washington, D.C. Dee (1907–1983) was from a family well-known in their local area as singers; his main source of ballads was his father, Daniel, who learned most of his songs prior to his marriage in 1887. Dee knew 400-plus songs, of which this one was both his and, according to Dee, his father's personal favorite. Dee was not averse to changing words or phrases in the pieces he knew, whenever he was unfamiliar with the meaning of a word he often changed it to suit his own purposes. Thus, the first verse he sang speaks of "around financher cottage homes" whereas other family members sang the line as "around their cottage firesides."

The second text was sent to me August 21, 1985, by Mrs. Attie Hart Dillingham of Plano, Texas. Mrs. Dillingham was born in Kentucky in 1899 and lived in Fayetteville, Arkansas, from 1956 to 1959 where she came to the attention of Mary Celestia Parler, then teaching folklore at the University of Arkansas. Parler recorded several of the songs in Dillingham's repertoire, and these tapes are still available at the University of Arkansas Library. Mrs. Dillingham learned "The Vulture of the Alps" from her father, who had it from his family. This dates it back roughly to the 1880s, or about the same time Daniel Hicks learned his version of the ballad. Although Mrs. Dillingham did not sing the ballad for me or send a music transcription, she did indicate that "it has a rather mournful melody, rising on the last half of stanza."

Ballads of the Supernatural

The Devil's Nine Questions

COLLECTED BY GEORGE FOSS FROM MILDRED CREIGHTON, CARRIE, KENTUCKY, 1962.
TRANSCRIBED BY GEORGE FOSS.

If you can't answer my questions nine,
Sing ninety-nine and ninety.
Oh, you're not God's, you're one of mine,
And you're not the weaver's bonny.

Oh, what is higher than the tree?
Sing ninety-nine and ninety.
And what is deeper than the sea?
And you're not the weaver's bonny.

Oh, Heaven is higher than the tree,
Sing ninety-nine and ninety.
And Hell is deeper than the sea,
And I am the weaver's bonny.

Oh, what is whiter than milk?
Sing ninety-nine and ninety.
And what is softer than the silk?
And you're not the weaver's bonny.

Oh, snow is whiter than the milk,
Sing ninety-nine and ninety.
And down is softer than the silk,
And I am the weaver's bonny.

Oh, what is louder than the horn?
Sing ninety-nine and ninety.
And what is sharper than the thorn?
And you're not the weaver's bonny.

Oh, thunder is louder than the horn,
Sing ninety-nine and ninety.
And hunger's sharper then the thorn,
And I am the weaver's bonny.

116

Oh, what is heavier than the lead?
Sing ninety-nine and ninety.
And what is better than the bread?
And you're not the weaver's bonny.

Oh, grief is heavier than the lead,
Sing ninety-nine and ninety.
God's blessing's better than the bread,
And I am the weaver's bonny.

Now you have answered my questions nine,
Sing ninety-nine and ninety.
Oh, you are God's, you're none of mine,
And you are the weaver's bonny.

This is the ballad Francis James Child listed as number 1 in *The English and Scottish Popular Ballads* under the title "Riddles Wisely Expounded." In addition to the present title the ballad is also known traditionally as "The Devil and the Blessed Virgin Mary," "There Was a Man Lived in the West," and "The Three Riddles." The ballad has been collected from traditional singers from Maine to North Carolina, the first American reporting being in 1922 by Alfreda M. Peel, who recorded it from the singing of a Mrs. Rill Martin of Mechanicsburg, Virginia. This ballad has three story types that are found in America, all of them involving a riddling contest in which the Devil takes part. In some texts he is clearly identified as the Devil, although in others he is initially referred to as a knight or cavalier who, over the course of the ballad, is revealed to be the Devil. The present version is of the most popular story type, a second major type differing mainly in the Devil's refusal to let the girl go even though she correctly answers his questions. A third type differs considerably: The Devil is a cavalier who asks the questions of three pretty girls in search of a lover. The youngest, who knows the answers, wins the Devil.

Riddling encounters, such as that given here, have played an important part in popular story for centuries, dating back at least to Biblical times. A number of traditional ballads, such as "King John and the Bishop," "Captain Wedderburn's Courtship," and "Proud Lady Margaret," are based on this theme. Indeed, some of the riddles used in "Captain Wedderburn's Courtship" are found in "Riddles Wisely Expounded," to such an extent that versions of the two ballads are sometimes confused by traditional singers. The love of verbal duels or contests of wits as exemplified by riddling encounters is probably one of the main reasons for the popularity of this ballad, although there are other possibilities. One is that its lyrics are easy to remember; another is that traditional singers may like the point that the ballad seems to make, namely that ordinary folk are not so easily outwitted, not so stupid as they may at first appear.

Some reports date this ballad back to an Irish manuscript of the twelfth century but most authorities believe it to be more recent. Child's earliest text dates from the fifteenth century and Samuel Pepys included a broadside text in his seventeenth-century collection. The earliest example with music is found in Thomas D'Urfey's *Wit and Mirth: or Pills to Purge Melancholy* (1719–1720), where it appears as "A Riddle Wittily Expounded." The broadsides that D'Urfey took his copy from suggest the ballad be sung to the tune of "Lay the Bent to the Bonny Broom." Unfortunately, no contemporary version of this melody has survived but D'Urfey's ballad has the title as a refrain line. D'Urfey's melody, however, is derived largely from another seventeenth-century song known as "At Home Would I Be," "I Would I Were in My Own Country," "The Northern Lasses' Lamentation," and "The Oak and the Ash and the Bonny Ivy Tree."

Even the earliest known text, Child's A*, shows some confusion in that the villain first offers the maid all the wisdom of the world if she will be his "leman," then immediately proceeds to tell his riddles, threatening her that she will be his unless she can give correct answers. This contradiction suggests the possibility that even in the early fifteenth century the ballad was in oral tradition or, at least, harked back to an earlier, imperfectly understood manuscript. Possibly, as Bertrand Bronson suggests, the contradiction arises from "homiletic rehandling, out of memories of Christ's temptation." The Child A* text indicates that the element of amorous appeal was found in the ballad at a very early date, even if it was not present in the original.

Although most texts have three, or some multiple of three (such as nine), questions, there are in the several known versions a total of thirty-two question asked. Among the more popular of these are "What is blacker than the raven?" (death), "What is darker than the night?" (a lie), "What is whiter than the snow?" (truth), "What is deeper than the sea?" (Hell), "What is greener than the grass?" (envy, poison), "What is louder than a horn?" (rumor, thunder), "What is sharper than a thorn?" (hunger), "What is rounder than a ring?" (the world), "What is whiter than milk?" (snow), "What is softer than silk?" (down), "What is higher than a tree?" (Heaven), "What is more innocent than a lamb?" (a baby), and "What is swifter (or faster) than the wind?" (thought).

The present text was collected in 1962 by George Foss from Mildred Creighton, Carrie, Kentucky. Foss was a prolific collector in the 1950s and 1960s who spent several months doing fieldwork in Kentucky, North Carolina, Virginia, and other parts of the South. Creighton was one of several traditional singers he recorded while spending time in Knott County, Kentucky, in the early 1960s.

The False Knight upon the Road

COLLECTED BY ANNABEL MORRIS BUCHANAN AND RICHARD CHASE FROM MRS. MAUD GENTRY LONG, HOT SPRINGS, NORTH CAROLINA, JUNE 28, 1936. TRANSCRIPTION BY ANNABEL MORRIS BUCHANAN AND RICHARD CHASE.

"Where are you going?" said the knight in the road.
"I'm going to my school," said the child as he stood.
He stood and he stood,
He well thought on he stood,
"I'm going to my school,"
Said the child as he stood.

"Oh, what do you study there?" said the knight in the road.
"We learn the word of God," said the child as he stood.
 He stood and he stood,
 He well thought on he stood,
 "We learn the word of God,"
 Said the child as he stood.

"I wish I were in the sea," said the knight in the road.
"A good boat under me," said the child as he stood.
 He stood and he stood,
 He well thought on he stood,
 "A good boat under me,"
 Said the child as he stood.

"I wish you were in the well," said the knight in the road.
"And you that deep in hell," said the child as he stood.
 He stood and he stood,
 He well thought on he stood,
 "And you that deep in hell,"
 Said the child as he stood.

The earliest report of this ballad is in 1827 when three versions, one with a melody line, were printed in William Motherwell's *Minstrelsy: Ancient and Modern.* All of these texts are Scottish and seem to provide conclusive evidence that the song originated in Scotland. Even though it is relatively rare the ballad has migrated to Nova Scotia, Maine, Indiana, Arkansas, Missouri, Kentucky, and Virginia. Listed under the present title as Child 3, the song is also known traditionally as "The Boy and the Devil," "False Fidee," "Fause Knicht and the Wee Boy," "The Devil and the School Child," "The False Knight to the Row," and "The Nightman." There are only two basic story types, both of which involve a contest of wits between a child, sometimes a boy and sometimes a girl, and a "false knight" (i.e., the Devil). The first type ends with the child naming the questioner while the second ends with the child throwing the questioner in a well. In neither type is much revealed about either the setting or situation.

The child is never supplied a name, being merely referred to as a child, wee lad, or a wee boy. The various known versions offer very little variety in the questions asked. The false knight usually wants to know where the child is going, what he has on his back, in his arm, who owns the sheep on a nearby hill, how many belong to him (i.e., the Devil), and the like; the knight then proceeds to express desires that the child be in a nearby tree with a ladder that breaks beneath him, that the child be on the sea in a ship that sinks with him. To each question and wish the child has a ready rejoinder and, of course, bests the knight. Because of the similar stories in the two ballads it is not surprising to know that some singers have confused this song with "Riddles Wisely Expounded."

The present text was collected June 28, 1936, by Richard Chase and Annabel Morris Buchanan from Mrs. Maud Gentry Long, Hot Springs, North Carolina. Both the informant and the collectors are well-known in Appalachian studies. Maud Long was the daughter of Mrs. Jane Gentry, who contributed significant numbers of ballads to Cecil Sharp and an equally important number of what she called "Old Jack, Will, and Tom Tales" to Isabel Gordon Carter, the first person to collect European wonder and magic tales in the southern Appalachians. Chase (1904–) is a former schoolteacher primarily known for his publication of versions of *The Jack Tales* retold in his own words (1943). Buchanan (1888–1978) was a native of Texas who spent most of her life in Virginia and Kentucky and is best known today for her work with the White Top (Virginia) Folk Festival of the 1930s. Mrs. Long learned the version of "False Knight" that Buchanan and Chase recorded from her mother, who sang it for Cecil Sharp in 1916. Melodically the main difference between Long's and Gentry's rendition is that Gentry's was in the key of F while Long's was in D. They also differ slightly textually, Long replacing Gentry's question "What are you eating?" with "What do you study there?" Undoubtedly a detailed study of the melodic and textual differences in the songs Gentry and Long both contributed to collectors would reveal much about the ways traditional balladry changes within families. Their family is one of the few for which sufficient material exists which one could use to make a meaningful study of this type.

Although the text given here seems incomplete there is no indication that the singer ever knew more of the ballad than this. In this particular instance it seems likely that had Long forgotten part of it the fact would have been noted, for other songs in the Buchanan-Chase collection have notes like, "This is all the singer could recall." Actually, the lack of a strong narrative is typical of versions of "The False Knight" that have been collected from traditional singers. In other words, Long's is as complete a variant as any of this particular ballad.

The House Carpenter's Wife

4th verse - the two line stanza

COLLECTED DECEMBER 1979 BY W.K. MCNEIL FROM NOBLE COWDEN, CUSHMAN,
ARKANSAS. TRANSCRIPTION BY W.K. MCNEIL.

Well met, well met, well met, said he,
Well met, well met, said she,
For I have come to these hilly lands
And it's all for the sake of thee;
For I have come to these hilly lands
And it's all for the sake of thee.

Well, you have married a house carpenter,
And a fine looking gentleman is he,
If you will leave the house carpenter
And run away with me
I'll take you to the place where the grass grows tall,
To the rivers of Sweet Willie.

She picked it up, her darling little babe,
And kisses gave it three,
Saying, stay at home you darlin' little babe,
For to keep your papa company.
Saying, stay at home you darlin' little babe,
For to keep your papa company.

And away went the sailor with the house carpenter's wife
To the rivers of Sweet Willie.

They hadn't been on the sea two weeks
I'm sure it was not three
'Til this young lady were a found weepin'
She was weepin' most bitterly.
'Til this young lady were a found weepin'
She was weepin' most bitterly.

Oh, is it for my gold you weep,
Or is it for my store,
Or is it for that house carpenter
That you never will see any more?
Or is it for that house carpenter
That you never will see any more?

It is not for your gold I weep,
Nor it is not for your store,
It's only for that darlin' little babe
That I never will see any more.
It's only for that darlin' little babe
That I never will see any more.

What is those banks, those banks I see
That look as white as snow?
It is the banks of Heaven I know,
Where my darlin' little babe shall go.
It is the banks of Heaven I know
Where my darlin' little babe shall go.

Oh, what is those banks, those banks I see
That looks so dark and low?
It is the banks of Hell I know,
Where you and I must go.
It is the banks of Hell I know,
Where you and I must go.

They had not been on the sea three weeks,
I'm sure it was not four,
Until from the deck there sprung a leak
And their voices wasn't heard any more.
Until from the deck there sprung a leak
And their voices wasn't heard any more.

Oh, cursed be the sea-sailing men,
Oh, cursed be their lives,
For robbing of little house carpenters,
And a-stealin' away their wives.
For robbing of little house carpenters,
And a-stealin' away their wives.

The House Carpenter

COLLECTED BY MERCEDES STEELY FROM MRS. NORA JOHNSON, EBENEZER, NORTH CAROLINA, APRIL 1935. TRANSCRIPTION BY MERCEDES STEELY.

"Well met, well met, well met," says he,
"Well met, true-lovers again.
For I am just from the salt-water sea,
And it's all for the sake of thee."

"Wunst I could've married a king's daughter dear,
And she would've married me,
But I refused her pairoom of gold;
It was all for the sake of thee."

"Well, if you could've married a king's daughter dear,
I surely think you to blame,
For I have married a house carpenter,
And I think he's a nice young man."

"Will you forsake your house carpenter
And go away with me?
I'll carry you where the grass grows green
On the banks of the sweet ivory."

She dressed all in her rich array,
She looked almost behold;
And every city that she went through,
She shined the same as gold.

She pickit up her lonesome little baby
And kissed it twicet or three:
"Lie here, lie here, my lonesome little baby,
And keep your papa comp'ny."

"Are you grieving for your silver or your gold,
Are you grieving for your store,
Are you grieving for your house carpenter
That you never shall see no mo'?"

124

"I'm neither grieving for my silver or my gold,
Nor I'm neither grieving for my store,
But I'm a grieving for my house carpenter,
And my sweetest little baby, too."

She hadn't been on deck more than two weeks or three,
I'm sure it was not four,
Before she began to weep and mourn
And wish she was back at home.

She walked them decks both night and day;
She cursed the sailors blue
For robbing her of her house carpenter
And her sweetest little baby, too.

The House Carpenter

COLLECTED BY MERCEDES STEELY FROM MRS. REBECCA JONES, EBENEZER, NORTH CAROLINA, MAY 1933. TRANSCRIPTION BY MERCEDES STEELY.

"I once could have married a king's daughter dear,
When she looked more wonderful sweet,
And she ran away with a house carpenter,
And she stayed with him three weeks."

"Who will forsaken the house carpenter,
Who will forsaken the land,
Who will forsaken all other things   ·
And go with you, young man?"

Says, "I will forsaken my house carpenter,
I will forsake my land,
I will forsaken all other things,
And I'll go with you, young man."

So she picked up her sweet little babe,
She kissed it more wonderful sweet;
Says, "Stay here with your pa, my dear,
He will keep you a-plenty to eat."

So they traveled on till bout three weeks,
Three weeks, I'm sure 'twas not four,
When there she wiped her water-weeping eyes,
And then she began to mourn.

" 'S air you weeping for my gold," says he,
"Air you weeping for my store,
Air you weeping for your house carpenter,
Which you never 'spec' to see any more?"

126

"I'm not weeping for your gold," says she,
"Neither am I for your store,
But I am weeping for my sweet little babe,
Which I never 'spec' to see any more."

So they traveled on till they come to the sea,
Where it looked more wonderful deep;
There she sprang a leap to the bottom of this boat,
And she sank for to rise no more.

'S I have seen green grass that were trod underfoot;
Soon it would spring and grow,
But here she sprang a leap to the bottom of this boat,
And she sank for to rise no more.

J'ai Marié un Ouvrier
(I Married a Carpenter)

COLLECTED IN 1934 BY ALAN LOMAX FROM LANESE VINCENT AND SIDNEY RICHARD, KAPLAN, LOUISIANA. TRANSCRIPTION BY DREW BEISSWENGER.

"J'ai marié un ouvrier, moi qui étais si vaillante fille,
Mais c'était de m'en dispenser sans attraper des reproches."

"Mais quitte ton ouvrier, et viens-t-en donc, c'est avec moi.
O vien-t-en donc, c'est avec moi dessus l'écore du Tennessee."

"Dessus l'écore du Tennessee, quoi-ce t'aurais pour m'entretenir?
Quoi-ce t'aurais pour m'entretenir dessus l'écore du Tennessee?"

"J'en ai de ces gros navires qui naviguent dessus l'eau
Et soi-disant pour t'opposer de travailler."

Au bout de trois jours, trois jours et trois semaines,
O la belle se mit à pleurer l'ennui de sa famille.

"Ne pleure donc pas, la belle, je t'acheterai une robe de soie jaune
Qu'elle soit mais la couleur de l'or et de l'argent."

"Je ne pleure non pas ton or, ni ton or ni ton argent,
Mais je pleure ma famille que j'ai laissée là-bas."

"Je t'ai pas toujours dit, la belle, et quand ce batiment calerait,
O il aurait une carlet à plus jamais resourdre.

"Dessus l'écore du Tennessee, t'embrasserais ton cher et petit bebe.
O tu l'embrasserais à plus jamais le revoir."

"I married a carpenter, I who was a girl of such means,
But how could I be rid of him without reproach?"

"Well, leave your carpenter, and come along with me.
O come along with me on the banks of the Tennessee."

"On the banks of the Tennessee, what would you have to provide
    for me?
What would you have to provide for me on the banks of
    the Tennessee?"

"I have great ships which sail the seas
And supposedly to keep you from ever working."

After three days, three days and three weeks,
O the lady began to weep out of longing for her family.

"Don't cry, Lady, I'll buy you a dress of yellow silk
The color of gold and silver."

"I do not weep for your gold, neither your gold nor your silver,
But I weep for my family that I left behind."

"Didn't I always tell you, Lady, that when this ship would sink,
O its mast would never again resurface.

"On the banks of the Tennessee, you would like your dear little baby.
O you would kiss him, never to see him again."

The texts given here are all variants of "James Harris, or the Daemon Lover" (Child 243), one of the most popular of the Child ballads in American tradition. Child's versions tell the story of Jane Reynolds and a sailor, James Harris, who exchange marriage vows. Harris is then pressed into service and, after three years, is reported dead. Jane then marries a ship carpenter, and they have children and live happily for four years. One night when her husband is away, Harris, in spirit form, raps at her window and says he has come to claim his love after seven long years. She goes with him because he claims he can support her well. She usually repents on shipboard but the boat sinks and she dies. Her husband never learns exactly what happened to her but hangs himself.

In America, the lover and the wife are usually unnamed and the carpenter is a "house" carpenter rather than a "ship" carpenter. The scenes before the arrival of the spirit and the aftermath dealing with the death of the carpenter are generally omitted. The supernatural elements of the English versions are played down although several of the American versions retain the "hills of Heaven" motif minus the eerie lover's cloven foot (a mark of the Devil). In these regards the first text given here is typical of other American examples but, musically, the variant is unusual, sounding far more modern than most other recorded versions of the ballad. Nevertheless, it is several generations old, for the informant learned it as a little girl. She recalls that it was one of the favorites that she and the other children in the family always asked their mother to sing.

It is not surprising that a ballad as popular as this one is in folk tradition has acquired many different titles. In addition to the titles given here and the one found in Child it is also known as "The Banks of Claudy," "The Faithless Wife," "Little Closet Door," "My Own True Love," "On the Banks of the Sweet Willie," "Said an Old True Love," "The Salt, Salt Sea," "The Salt Water Sea," "The Sea Captain," "Sweet Wilder," "A Warning for Married Women," "Young Turtle Dove," "Fair Janie," "The King's Daughter," "Nice Young Man," "Sweet William," "Well Met, We're Met, We're Met," and "The Young Ship's Carpenter." This rather extensive list could easily be lengthened by several additional titles, so the point is amply demonstrated that there is not only great variation in the text of this ballad but in its title as well.

The first text here was collected by W.K. McNeil in December 1979 from Noble Cowden, Cushman, Arkansas. She was born June 28, 1906, one of several children of a singing family. Both her father, Albert Bullard, and her mother, Saphronia, knew many old British ballads and were Noble's main source of songs. Several of these numbers are now known by Mrs. Cowden's children and grandchildren although none of them has as extensive a repertoire as Noble does. She has on occasion performed at the Arkansas Traveler Folk Theater at Hardy, Arkansas, and at the Ozark Folk Center, Mountain View, Arkansas, but mainly she sings her songs for herself and her family. A rather retiring person, Noble is among the best contemporary Ozark folksingers.

The second text was collected in April 1935 by Mercedes Steely from Mrs. Nora Johnson, Ebenezer, North Carolina. Mrs. Johnson learned the ballad during her childhood from her cousin Lem Moore. The third text was also collected by Mercedes Steely, from Mrs. Rebecca Jones, Ebenezer, North Carolina, in May 1933. Mrs. Jones learned the ballad as a child but her exact source is not identified.

The fourth text here is a Louisiana French version collected by Alan Lomax in 1934 from Lanese Vincent and Sidney Richard, Kaplan, Louisiana. One Sunday afternoon, Wilfred Hebert overheard Lomax talking about his fieldwork and told him that Vincent and Richard, who were in town for a visit, often sang for weddings and other social gatherings. When Lomax found them, they refused at first, explaining that they were not in the mood, but after a few drinks, they agreed to sing a few songs. To escape the noise of the street, they all went inside one of the Louisiana State rice mill chutes and recorded six songs. Vincent and Richard were from a family of singers, parents, aunts, uncles, cousins and grandparents who all celebrated holidays and special events with ancient songs about tragedy and treachery. They even sang unaccompanied songs during breaks at house dances.

In Louisiana an *ouvrier* is not a general laborer, as is the case in France, but specifically a carpenter. In this version, a well-bred young wife, bored with her carpenter husband, is swept away by a sailor. When he brings her to the port city, she learns that she is to sail with him. She then realizes that she will never return to the family she has abandoned. The yellow silk dress he offers her in consolation is mentioned in Scottish versions of the ballad. She then learns that they are to leave and the ship is to sink. Apparently, however, she will be allowed to kiss her beloved child farewell before going on to meet her ultimate fate. As is true of American versions generally, the demon nature of her lover is not fully developed. He seems to be simply a rake. Although it is tempting to explore the connection between Breton France and Celtic England, it is more likely that this Louisiana French variant was translated from American sources. In his notes, Child refers to an Americanized version published in Philadelphia in 1858 which mentions "the banks of the old Tennessee." (See volume 4 of the Dover edition, p. 361.)

Lazarus

COLLECTED APRIL 16, 1965, BY CHARLENE CURETON FROM A WOMAN IDENTIFIED ONLY AS MRS. HOGAN, NEWPORT, TENNESSEE. TRANSCRIPTION BY ANNETTE WOLFORD.

There was a little family
That lived in Bethany;
Two sisters and their brother
Composed a family.

They lived in peace and pleasure
For a many a long years;
They laid away their treasures
Beyond this vale of tears.

Yet, while they lived so happy,
So pure, so kind and good,
Their brother was afflicted
And rued life throned in bed.

The news came to the sisters,
Laid Lazarus in the tomb
And prayed for to comfort
And drive away their gloom.

When Jesus heard the tidings
Low in the distant land,
So slowly did he travel
To meet that lonely band.

When Jesus was a-coming,
Mary met Him on the way
And told Him how her brother
Had died and passed away.

He cheered her and He blessed her
And told her not to weep,
For in Him was the power
To wake him from his sleep.

132

When He was coming nigher,
Marthy ran and met Him too
And at his feet a-weeping
Rehearsed the tale of woe.

When Jesus saw her weeping,
He fell a-weeping too
And wept until they showed him
Where Lazarus laid in tomb.

He rolled away the cover
And walked upon the ground
Within full life and vigor
He walked upon the ground.

So if we but love Jesus
And do His Holy will,
Like Marthy and Mary
And Lazarus use it well,

From death He will redeem us
And take us to the sky
And bid us live forever
Where pleasure never dies.

This song is one of the few biblical ballads to be found in American folk tradition. Although similar in theme to a seventeenth-century British ballad, this is apparently a native American product. The earliest report of the piece is a manuscript copy in Belden's collection that is dated August 21, 1865. George Pullen Jackson noted a copy dated 1871 in a songbook published by a C.L. McConnell that credits the ballad to an Elder E.D. Thomas of Catlettsburg, Kentucky. Both Belden and Jackson suggested that print played a large part in perpetuating and propagating the song but were unable to turn up much evidence to support their assumption. No one can honestly deny that the ballad is widely known for it has been collected from traditional singers in Michigan, Missouri, North Carolina, West Virginia, Ohio, Tennessee, Mississippi, Arkansas, Virginia, and Kentucky.

Besides "The Little Family," its most common title, and the one given here, the song is also known as "Family Lived in Bethany," "Mary, Martha and Lazarus," and "Martha and Mary" or "Mary and Martha." The present version was collected April 16, 1965, by Charlene Cureton from a woman identified only as Mrs. Hogan, Newport, Tennessee. Nothing further is given concerning either the collector or informant.

Mary Hebrew

COLLECTED BY BEN GRAY LUMPKIN FROM MRS. PEARL HARTSELL, CHAPEL HILL,
NORTH CAROLINA, SEPTEMBER 1951. TRANSCRIBED BY HELEN KAY WILSON.

Mary Hebrew had three little babes,
And she sent them off to school.
She sent them away to a foreign land
To learn their grammaries.

They hadn't been gone but a very short time,
About three months and a day,
When a hurricane came all over the land
And swept her babes away.

"O, King in Heaven," aloud she cried—
"The King who wears the crown—
Come bring me home my three little babes,
Tonight or in the morning soon."

It was not long, about Christmas time,
When the nights grew long and cool,
Come flying home her three little babes
Unto their mother's room.

She fixed a table in the hall,
And on it put bread and wine.
"Come on and eat, my three little babes;
Come eat and drink o' my wine."

"O, we'll eat none of your bread, Mother dear,
But we'll drink none of your wine;
For yonder stands our Savior dear,
And shortly we must go."

She fixed the bed in the back side room,
And on it put a clean sheet.
And on the top spread a golden cloth,
For her three babes to sleep.

"Rise up, rise up," cried the eldest one.
"For the pinions're growing strong,
And yonder stands our Savior dear,
And shortly we must go.

"Dark clouds of dirt are at our head.
Grass grows at our feet.
You've shed enough tears for us, Mother dear,
To wet our winding sheet."

This ballad is usually known as "The Wife of Usher's Well," the title used by Francis J. Child, who included it as number 79 in his ten-volume work *The English and Scottish Popular Ballads*. Although of British origin the song seems to have survived better in the United States than in the old country, most reported versions being from the American South. The earliest known printing of the ballad is in Sir Walter Scott's *Minstrelsy of the Scottish Border* (1802), and thus it dates from at least the latter half of the eighteenth century and is possibly even older.

American versions generally differ from British ones in the following ways: (1) the revenants are children, frequently girls, rather than grown boys; (2) the cursing of the waters episode is omitted, but the mother usually prays for the return of her children; (3) the ghosts refuse earthly pleasures in many cases because the Savior stands yonder; (4)the ghosts are not recalled at the crowing of the cocks; (5) the children leave home to learn their grammarie; and (6) the folk belief that tears for the dead wet the winding sheets and disturb the peace is present. "Grammarie" is an obsolete word meaning either general knowledge or magic. The ghostly nature of the children is frequently assumed without actually being stated.

The lyrics given here differ from most in that it is suggested that the children return as angels rather than ghosts. Also unusual is the use of the word *pinions* in stanza 8; according to the informant it referred to "angel's wings." There is, of course, the possibility that the presence of *pinions* in this version is merely an accident of oral transmission but it could also be a survival from an old version in which the children clearly return as angels. The present text was collected in September 1951 by Ben Gray Lumpkin from Mrs. Pearl Hartsell, Chapel Hill, North Carolina. She learned this song and others in her repertoire about 1915 from her mother, Mrs. Henry Connell, and her grandmother, Mrs. James Taylor Burris, both from Stanly County, North Carolina.

Two Brothers

COLLECTED SEPTEMBER 3, 1965, BY GEORGE FOSS FROM MARY WOODS SHIFLETT, BROWNS COVE, VIRGINIA. TRANSCRIPTION BY DAN BRACKIN.

There was two brothers in one schoolroom
One evening coming home.
The oldest said to the youngest one,
"Let's have a wrestle and fall."

The oldest threw the youngest one,
He threw him to the ground,
And out of his pocket he drew a penknife,
He gave him a deathly wound.

"Pull off, pull off your woolen shirt
And tie it from gore to gore,
And wrap it around my bleeding wound
And it will bleed no more."

Oh, he pulled off his woolen shirt,
He tied it from gore to gore,
He wrapped it around his bleeding wound
And it did bleed no more.

"Take me up, take me up, upon your back
And carry me 'yond the churchyard,
And dig my grave both wide and deep
And gently lay me down."

"What must I tell your loving father
When he calls for his son John?"
"Tell him I'm in some lonely green woods
A-learning young hounds to run."

"What must I tell your loving mother
When she calls for her son John?"
"Tell her I'm in some graded school,
Good scholar never to return."

"What must I tell your loving Susie
When she calls for her dear John?"
"Tell her I'm in some lonely graveyard,
My books to carry back home."

When loving Susie heard of this
She got her horn and blew.
She charmed the birdies from the nest,
The fishes out of the sea.

She charmed little Johnny out of his grave,
Saying, "Susie what do you want?"
"Oh, one sweet kiss from your sweet lips
Is all my heart does care."

"Go home, go home my loving Susie
And weep no more for me.
For one sweet kiss from my sweet lips
Will cause your days short on."

This ballad, listed by Child as number 49, is better known in the United States than in its homeland. It is known under a variety of titles, including "As Two Little Schoolboys Were Going to School," "Billy Murdered John," "Brother's Murder," "The Dying Soldier," "Jessel Town," "John and William," "The Rolling of the Stones," "Take My Fine Shirt," and "Yonder School." In America five basic story types of the ballad are found, the main one being that given in the present text. Another type has the crime being accidental, while a third omits all mention of the love affair and the jealousy. A fourth story type has the narrative dealing with a battlefield scene, and in the fifth the murder happens as a result of spontaneous anger during a daylong test of strength between two brothers in the woods. In this last story type the mother is often implicated in the murder, a direct contradiction of the reasons for the crime. Thus, the principal difference between the story types is whether the murder is purposeful or accidental and whether or not it is the result of a love relationship.

Most American versions of "The Two Brothers" strip the ballad of much of its narrative by omitting the postburial scene between the two lovers. This is in keeping with the general American tendency to eliminate supernatural elements in Child ballads. Frequently the refusal to play baseball is the factor provoking the murder, but jealousy over a sweetheart is still the most common provocation. Southern texts are generally short, often no more than three to six verses long, a feature that in many cases may simply be due to forgetfulness on the part of the singers. Many of the published examples indicate that the informants realized that the ballad is longer than the text they have provided. Few, though, have been as explicit as Mrs. Mildred Tuttle of Farmington, Arkansas, who told Vance Randolph, "It was originally a long piece about a fool boy who murdered his brother with a pocket-knife, just because he did not feel like playing baseball."

While to some the theme of this ballad may seem too gory or violent for children's ears, it has throughout much of its history been popular as a children's song. In the 1880s William Wells Newell heard it at a picnic where a group of young girls was singing it. Mrs. Alice Best of Fox, Arkansas, from whom I collected a version of "Two Brothers" on April 25, 1979, recalls that the piece was very popular with her age group when she was a child in the 1890s. Undoubtedly, other evidence attesting to the popularity of "The Two Brothers" as a children's song would be known if most early folksong collectors had been interested in asking about such matters.

The present version of "Two Brothers" was collected September 3, 1965, by George Foss from Mary Woods Shiflett, Browns Cove, Virginia. Mrs. Shiflett was born in 1902 and at the time of collection had been widowed for several years. A very energetic person, she supported herself, until illness confined her to a Baltimore nursing home, by cutting timber, running moonshine stills, making quilts, making apple butter, and housing up to a dozen welfare children at a time as foster parent. The exact source of her version of this ballad is not indicated, but it probably came from her family, who were well known locally for their singing.

Fair Margaret and Sweet William

COLLECTED SEPTEMBER 1, 1962, BY GEORGE FOSS FROM MAUD BOELYN, ARY, KENTUCKY. TRANSCRIPTION BY DAN BRACKIN.

Sweet William arose one May morning
And dressed hisself in blue.
"Pray tell unto me that love long lie
That's betwixt Lady Margaret and you."

"I know nothing about Lady Margaret's love,
I'm sure she don't love me.
But tomorrow morning at eight o'clock
Lady Margaret my bride shall see."

Lady Margaret was standing in her own hall door,
Combing back her hair,
And who did she spy but Sweet William and his bride
And the lawyers go riding by.

She threw away her ivory comb,
Bound up her head in silk,
And she stepped out of her own hall door,
Ne'er return any more.

Sweet William he said he was troubled in his head
From the dream he had dreamed last night.
He dreamed that his hall was filled with white swine
And his true love was swimming in blood.

"How do you like your bed?" said she,
"How do you like your sheet?
How do you like the pretty fair maid
That lies in your arms asleep?"

"Very well do I like my bed," said he,
"Much better I like my sheet.
But the best of them all is the pretty fair maid
That stands at my bed sheet."

He called them all around his bed,
He counted one, two, three.
He asked of them all and he asked of his bride
Lady Margaret he might go and see.

He rode and he rode till he came to the hall,
He jangled on the ring.
And none was so ready as Lady Margaret's brother
To rise and bid him come in.

"Is she in her kitchen?" said he,
"Or is she in her hall?
Or is she in her upper chamber
Among those ladies all?"

"She's neither in her kitchen," said he,
"She's neither in her hall,
But in yonder she lies in her clay cold coffin
A-setting against the wall."

"Unfold, unfold those winding sheets,
They're made of linen so fine.
And let me kiss them soft pale lips
That have so often kissed mine."

He kissed her on her lily-white cheek,
And then he kissed her chin,
And then he kissed her pretty white lips
That pierced his heart within.

"Fold back, fold back those winding sheets,
Let her lay in the linen so fine.
Today you stood over Lady Margaret's corpse
And tomorrow you'll stand over mine."

Lady Margaret was buried in the old churchyard,
Sweet William by her side.
And out of her breast sprang a red, red rose
And out of his sprang a brier.

They grew and they grew to the top of the church
They could not grow any higher.
They leaned till they tied in a true lover's knot,
The red rose around the green brier.

The first known printing of this piece is in Francis Beaumont and John Fletcher's play *The Knight of the Burning Pestle,* where it is quoted in two acts of the drama. Child listed it as number 74, under the present title, and it is among the more popular of his ballads in America. There are eight basic story types of the ballad as found in North America, none of which closely resembles any Child version. The first type is that given in the present text, and a second type is the same except that Margaret commits suicide onstage by jumping out of the window. A third type has William's bride having the dream and telling it to him. A fourth story type contains a description of Margaret's actions after she leaves the window; eventually she dies of a broken heart. In a fifth story type Margaret is still alive when she comes to the foot of William's bed, while a sixth story type eliminates the ghost. William goes to see Margaret who has died; he then dies but nothing grows from his grave. The rose growing from Margaret's grave dies after it reaches William's breast, and thus no lover's knot is tied. A seventh type has the ghost blessing the lovers before going to the grave; the song ends with Margaret's seven brothers refusing to let William see their sister. The final type has Marjorie leaping to her death after seeing Willie and his bride enter the church. The usual sequence with the ghost is given after Willie says he prefers Marjorie to his bride, the ghost strikes him on the breast with a comb that causes his death.

In North America the ballad is known by many titles, including "False William," "Lady Margaret," "Lady Maud's Ghost," "Lyddy Margot," "Pretty Polly and Sweet William," "Sweet William's Bride," and "William Hall." The dropping of the ghost from some versions is attributable to the general American tendency to eliminate supernatural elements. The woman's name changes more often than the man's. He is always named William or Willie, and while she is usually known as Margaret she is also called Polly, Maud, Maggie, Marget, and Margot—most of these names being very close to Margaret and, in some cases, probably a result of misunderstanding that name. Several American versions of the ballad show a tendency toward the spectacular, and contain very graphic descriptions of Lady Margaret's suicide. Although the "rose-briar" motif is most often associated with "Barbara Allen" it appears in some of Child's texts and was probably original to this ballad. However, it could have been appropriated from another song, as it is a relatively common ballad cliché. This ballad story is very dramatic and somewhat improbable, but the reasons for its widespread appeal are obvious. It has many of the narrative elements found in modern soap operas—adultery, highly emotional scenes, tragedy—some of which even include supernatural details.

An interesting version of this ballad was issued on Paramount Records in 1929. Performed by Dr. I. (Isaac) G. (Garfield) Greer (1881–

1967) and his wife, Willie Spainhour Greer, the version was titled "Sweet William and Fair Ellen" and is unusual for a number of reasons. It is one of the few texts in which the girl is named Ellen, the story line is drastically altered, and the narrative resembles another piece, of Irish origin, called "The Jolly Soldier." Greer, a native of Zionville, North Carolina, and his wife, a native of Boone, North Carolina, were among the earliest "professional" folk singers, their first concert being held at Appalachian State Teachers College (now Appalachian State University) in Boone, North Carolina, in 1917. Unlike some later "folk singers," the Greers did come from a strong traditional background.

The present version of "Fair Margaret and Sweet William" was collected September 1, 1962, by George Foss from Maud Boelyn, Ary, Kentucky.

The Seventh Sister

COLLECTED BY ANNABEL MORRIS BUCHANAN FROM MRS. CARRIE LOUISE BECK, HENDERSONVILLE, NORTH CAROLINA, JULY 7, 1954. TRANSCRIPTION BY ANNABEL MORRIS BUCHANAN.

"Come rise you up, my pretty fair maid,
　　Come ride along with me,
We'll ride the length of this long summer's morn,
　　And married we shall be, be,
　　And married we shall be."

He mounted on the milk-white horse,
　　And she on the dapple-grey,
They rode the length of a long summer's morn,
　　Till they came to the rolling sea, sea,
　　Till they came to the rolling sea.

"Light down, light down, my pretty fair maid,
　　Light down, light down," says he,
"Six of your sisters I've drowned here,
　　And the seventh one you shall be, be,
　　And the seventh one you shall be.

"Take off, take off those satin robes
　　And hang them on yonder's rock,
For they are too pretty and they are too good
　　To lay in the sea and rot, rot,
　　To lay in the sea and rot."

"Turn your face to-ward the wood,
　　And turn your back on me;
I never thought that a naked woman
　　Was fitten for a man to see, see,
　　Was fitten for a man to see."

He turned his face to-ward the wood,
    He turned his back on me;
I caught him around his waist so small,
    And slung him in yonder sea, sea,
    And slung him in yonder sea.

She mounted on the milk-white horse,
    Leading the dapple-grey,
And when she reached her father's house
    It was just three hours till day, day,
    It was just three hours till day.

"Oh, shut your mouth, you parrot bird,
    Don't tell no tales on me,
And your cage shall be made of gold and silver,
    And hung on the willow tree, tree,
    And hung on the willow tree."

Child commented that "of all ballads this has perhaps attained the widest circulation" (I, p. 22). He was referring only to Europe but his remarks apply equally well to America for even today this is one of the favorite Child ballads. Indeed, Bertrand Bronson lists this as the fourth most popular of the Child ballads (see *The Ballad as Song* (Berkeley: University of California Press, 1969), pp. 165–66). Child listed it as number 4 under the title "Lady Isabel and the Elf-Knight" but it is known traditionally under numerous titles. These include "The Outlandish Knight," "Billy Came Over the Main White Ocean," "The Cage of Ivory and Gold," "Castle By the Sea," "The Daughter of Old England," "The Errant Knight," "The False-Hearted Knight," "The False Lover," "Go Steal to Me Your Father's Gold," "He Followed Me Up and He Followed Me Down," "If I Take Off My Silken Stay," "Little Golden," "The Knight of the Northland," "A Man in the Land," "Miss Mary's Parrot," "The Ocean Wave," "The Gates of Ivory," "and almost as many more different titles. The ballad has been reported from most of the Southern states as well as in New York, Maine, Missouri, Indiana, Colorado, West Virginia, Ohio, Vermont, Michigan, Utah, Pennsylvania, and Oklahoma. In addition it has been collected in Nova Scotia, Newfoundland, and Ontario, and it may even be more widely known than this list indicates.

Seven story types of the ballad exist in American tradition. In the most popular of these a knight convinces a family's seventh daughter to rob her parents and elope with him. He takes her to the place where he has drowned her six sisters and asks her to remove her valuable robe before he kills her. She asks him to turn around so he will not see her

---

*Or "Six fair maidens I've drowned here"

144

naked, and when he does she pushes him in the stream to drown. She then returns home and replaces the money, after which a parrot questions her concerning her activities. By promising an elaborate cage, the girl convinces him not to tell on her. Therefore, when the king asks the parrot about the fuss, he says a cat has been around the cage. This is essentially the narrative given in the present version except that the robbery is omitted and the dialogue with the parrot is attenuated. A second type makes the knight's supernatural nature very clear, while in a third type the parrot accuses the girl of the murder. A fourth story type has the parrot failing in his attempt to deceive the girl's father. In a fifth story type the episode of the knight's drowning is protracted. After the girl removes her robe the knight drags her into the water but, by some means, he drowns. She then returns home where her mother and the parrot have the usual conversation about the cat. In a sixth story type the parrot is missing and in a seventh both the parrot and the father are missing. When the girl returns home she prays to God, thanking him for her escape.

Although the earliest reports of this ballad are from the seventeenth century, it is thought by some to be an offshoot of the biblical story of Judith and Holofernes, a suggestion Child rejected. He did agree that the story belonged to a large body of European tales and hypothesized "that an independent European tradition existed of a half-human, half-demonic being, who possessed an irresistible power of decoying away young maids, and was wont to kill them after he got them into his hands, but who at last found one who was more than his match, and lost his own life through her craft and courage. A modification of this story is afforded by the large class of Bluebeard tales" (1, p. 54). Others have traced the false knight back to a twelfth-century demon king of the Lower Rhine region. Whatever its origins, there can be little doubt that nineteenth-century English broadsides played a large part in keeping the ballad alive in the British Isles, for it was a favorite with broadside printers of the era. These texts generally consisted of three scenes: (1) the knight cajoling the girl, (2) the waterside, and (3) the parrot.

In most American versions neither the villain nor the heroine is named, but when they are Mary and Polly are the most common names for the girl while William and John are the most favored names for the knight. In a number of American lyrics the girl and the parrot have the same name (Polly), which tends to make the story hard to follow. The knight's supernatural character is missing, which is hardly surprising since such elements generally tend to disappear in American renditions of Old World ballads. It is also characteristic of American texts that the girl is very vigorous. In one version she throws a rock at the drowning knight and in the text given here she doesn't just push him into the water, she "slung him in yonder sea."

If any proof of the ballad's popularity were needed it is provided in the large number of parodies that have cropped up over the years. Some of these appeared in minstrel show songbooks during the nineteenth century. The narrative also exists as a folktale in both prose and cante fable form. The present version of the ballad was collected July 7, 1954, by Annabel Morris Buchanan from Carrie Louise Thames (Mrs. D.G.) Beck, Hendersonville, North Carolina. For more information about Buchanan see the notes for "The False Knight upon the Road." For more about Beck see the notes for "Miss Mary Belle." She learned "The Seventh Sister" as a child in South Carolina from her mother, Evelyn Roberson Thames, who was a native of Canada.

Sonny Hugh

COLLECTED BY BEN GRAY LUMPKIN FROM MRS. PEARL HARTSELL, CHAPEL HILL, NORTH CAROLINA, SEPTEMBER 1951. TRANSCRIBED BY HELEN KAY WILSON.

'T was on a holly summer day.
Not a drop of dew had fell.
"I've come to play, boys!"
A-tossing their balls around, around, around.
A-tossing their balls around.

They tossed them high; they tossed them low.
They tossed them over the garden wall.
They tossed them over into Jewry's yard,
Where no one was allowed to go, go, go,
Where no one was allowed to go.

There came a lady to the door,
All dressed in silk and white.
"Come in, little boy; you shall have your ball.
You shall have your ball tonight, tonight, tonight.
You shall have your ball tonight.

"I can't come in. I shan't come in,
Unless my playmates come with me;
For everyone that ever went in
That ever came out again, gain, gain.
That ever came out again."

She first showed him a big red apple.
Then she showed him a cherry.
Then she showed him a gold charm ring,
Which enticed the little boy in, in, in.
Which enticed the little boy in.

She took him by his little white hand.
She led him through the hall.
She led him into a back side room,
Where no one could hear him call, call, call,
Where no one could hear him call.

147

She placed him down in an easy chair.
She pierced him with her pin.
And in her bowl, her silver bowl,
She led his heart's blood in, in, in.
She led his heart's blood in.

His mother walking up and down,
With hickories in her hand.
"If only I could find my little Sonny Hugh,
O, how I'd whip him home, home, home.
O, how I'd whip him home.

She walked till she came to that great well
Which was so deep and cold.
"If you are here, my little Sonny Hugh,
I wish you'd speak to me, me, me.
I wish you'd speak to me.

"I am here, O Mother dear.
I've been right here so long.
The pin she ran right through my heart.
The red blood runs so strong, strong, strong.
The red blood runs so strong.

"Go bury my Bible at my head.
My songbook at my feet.
And, if any of my playmates ask for me,
Pray tell them that I'm asleep, sleep, sleep.
Pray tell them that I'm asleep."

It is generally accepted that this ballad is based on an incident that may have occurred in 1255. Francis J. Child, who included the ballad as number 155 in his *The English and Scottish Popular Ballads* under the title "Sir Hugh; of The Jew's Daughter," gives the story (III, p. 235) as related in the *Annals of Waverly* (1219–1266):

A boy in Lincoln, named Hugh, was crucified by the Jews in contempt of Christ, with various preliminary tortures. To conceal the act from the Christians, the body, when taken from the cross, was thrown into a running stream; but the water would not endure the wrong done its maker, and immediately ejected it upon dry land. The body was then buried in the earth, but was found above dry ground the next day. The guilty parties were now very much frightened and quite at their wit's end; as a last resort they threw the corpse into a drinking well. The body was seen floating on the water, and upon its being drawn up, the hands and feet were found to be pierced, the head had, as it were, a crown of bloody points, and there were various other wounds: from all which it was plain that this was the work of the abominable Jews. A blind woman, touching the bier on which the blessed martyr's corpse was carrying to the church, received her sight, and many other miracles followed. Eighteen Jews, convicted of the crime, and confessing it with their own mouth, were hanged.

Matthew Paris, also writing contemporaneously, added several details, including that of the mother's finding of the child, which figures prominently in most ballad versions of the story. A long report on the case is provided in *The Annals of Burton,* a manuscript compiled primarily in the fourteenth century. Chaucer referred to the murder of Sir Hugh of Lincoln in "The Prioress's Tale," and the crime was the subject of numerous ballads in French and English. Many of the latter were collected in a small volume published in Paris in 1834.

Although folksong specialists usually refer to the ballad by the title Child used, it has many other traditional titles. These include "The Blue Drum Boy," "Hugh of Lincoln," "It Rained a Mist," "The Jew's Garden," "A Little Boy Lost His Ball," "So High," "Once in the Month of May," "Water Birch," "Fatal Flower Garden," " 'Twas on a Cold and Winter's Day," and, of course, the present "Sonny Hugh," among others. It is not only the title that has undergone great change; the lyrics also show great variation in America. In many versions the religious note is all but forgotten. In one text reported from Florida the girl is a jeweler's daughter and in a Mississippi version the Jew is stripped of religious identity and is just "a man." In some versions the boy is killed by his aunt or his mother. A "duke's" or a "king's daughter" or a "mother's maid" figures prominently in some texts; in others the crime takes place in a "queen's garden" and is committed by a "gypsy." In some versions "Jew," "Hugh," and "Dew" have been confused, and thus in a Tennessee text the boy is identified both as "Hugh" and "Dew" at different points in the song. He is murdered by a "Miss Dew" in the garden of the Dew family. Elements from other Child ballads crop up occasionally, as in one version where the boy promises to marry Barbary Ellen when he grows up.

The present version was collected in September 1951 by Ben Gray Lumpkin from Mrs. Pearl Hartsell, Chapel Hill, North Carolina. For more information about Mrs. Hartsell see the headnotes for "Mary Hebrew." Her lyrics differ from most in stating that "not a drop of dew had fell," most texts being set in a rainy day. Also Mrs. Hartsell sings of the mother setting out with "hickories in her hand" rather than the pike-staff or little rod or sally rod of most versions. Mrs. Hartsell's text also provides a natural, yet poignantly ironical, note missing from other versions when she sings of the mother setting out to find her tardy son. She says, "If I could find my little Sonny Hugh,/O, how I'd whip him home."

The Two Sisters

COLLECTED BY GEORGE FOSS FROM MILDRED CREIGHTON, CARRIE, KENTUCKY, 1962.
TRANSCRIBED BY GEORGE FOSS.

> There lived an old lady by the Northern Sea,
>> Bow down,
>
> There lived an old lady by the Northern Sea,
>> The boughs they bend to me.
>
> There lived an old lord by the Northern Sea,
> And he had daughters one, two, three.
>> I will be true, true to my love,
>> Love and my love will be true to me.

150

A young man came a-courting there,
    Bow down,
A young man came a-courting there,
    The boughs they bend to me.
A young man came a-courting there,
And he took choice of the youngest there.
      I will be true, true to my love,
      Love and my love will be true to me.

He gave the youngest a gay gold ring,
    Bow down,
He gave the youngest a gay gold ring,
    The boughs they bend to me.
He gave the youngest a gay gold ring,
But never the oldest a single thing.
      I will be true, true to my love,
      Love and my love will be true to me.

He gave the youngest a beaver hat,
    Bow down,
He gave the youngest a beaver hat,
    The boughs they bend to me.
He gave the youngest a beaver hat,
The oldest she thought much of that.
      I will be true, true to my love,
      Love and my love will be true to me.

"Oh sister, oh sister let us walk out,"
    Bow down,
"Oh sister, oh sister let us walk out,"
    The boughs they bend to me.
"Oh sister, oh sister let us walk out,
And see the ships a-sailing about."
      I will be true, true to my love,
      Love and my love will be true to me.

On they walked down by the salty brim,
    Bow down,
They walked down by the salty brim,
    The boughs they bend to me.
On they walked down by the salty brim,
The oldest pushed the youngest in.
      I will be true, true to my love,
      Love and my love will be true to me.

"Oh sister, oh sister lend me your hand,"
    Bow down,
"Oh sister, oh sister lend me your hand,"
    The boughs they bend to me.
"Oh sister, oh sister lend me your hand,
And I will give you my house and land."
        I will be true, true to my love,
        Love and my love will be true to me.

"I'll lend you neither my hand nor glove,"
    Bow down,
"I'll lend you neither my hand nor glove,"
    The boughs they bend to me.
"I'll lend you neither my hand nor glove,
But I will have your own true love."
        I will be true, true to my love,
        Love and my love will be true to me.

Oh, down she sank and away she swam,
    Bow down,
Oh, down she sank and away she swam,
    The boughs they bend to me.
Oh, down she sank and away she swam,
And into the miller's fish pond she ran.
        I will be true, true to my love,
        Love and my love will be true to me.

The miller came out with his fish hook,
    Bow down,
The miller came out with his fish hook,
    The boughs they bend to me.
The miller came out with his fish hook,
And fished the fair maid out of the brook.
        I will be true, true to my love,
        Love and my love will be true to me.

He robbed her of her gay gold ring,
    Bow down,
He robbed her of her gay gold ring,
    The boughs they bend to me.
He robbed her of her gay gold ring,
And into the sea he pushed her again.
        I will be true, true to my love,
        Love and my love will be true to me.

The miller was hung at his mill gate,
    Bow down,
The miller was hung at his mill gate,
    The boughs they bend to me.
The miller was hung at his mill gate,
The oldest daughter was burned at the stake.
    I will be true, true to my love,
    Love and my love will be true to me.

The Two Sisters
(Wind and Rain)

COLLECTED BY GEORGE FOSS FROM DAN TATE, FANCY GAP, VIRGINIA, 1962.
TRANSCRIBED BY GEORGE FOSS.

Two loving sisters was a-walking side by side,
    Oh the wind and rain.
One pushed the other off in the waters, waters deep,
    And she cried, "The dreadful wind and rain."

She swum down, down to the miller's pond,
    Oh the wind and rain.
She swum down, down to the miller's, miller's pond,
    And she cried, "The dreadful wind and rain."

Out run the miller with his long hook and line,
    Oh the wind and rain.
Out run the miller with his long hook and line,
    And she cried, "The dreadful wind and rain."

He hooked her up by the tail of the gown,
    Oh the wind and rain.
He hooked her up by the tail of the gown,
    And she cried, "The dreadful wind and rain."

They made fiddle strings of her long black hair,
    Oh the wind and rain.
They made fiddle strings of her long black hair,
    And she cried, "The dreadful wind and rain."

They made fiddle screws of her long finger bones,
    Oh the wind and rain.
They made fiddle screws of her long finger bones,
    And she cried, "The dreadful wind and rain."

The only tune that my fiddle would play, was
    Oh the wind and the rain.
The only tune that my fiddle would play, was
    And she cried, "The dreadful wind and rain."

Under the title "The Two Sisters" Francis James Child listed this as number 10 in his *The English and Scottish Popular Ballads.* Popular in Europe as well as in the United States, this song has greater story variation than any other Child ballad. Twenty-one different story types exist. Most of them involve one sister drowning another (usually the older does the younger one in) but there are some variations on this situation. For example, a text in the *Bulletin of the Folk-Song Society of the Northeast* (XII, 10) has one of the girls killed by a man named Miller who then proceeds to make a fiddle of her body. The instrument made from the girl's body turns up in many versions, and in some it reveals the murderer. The miller is a central figure in most American versions; in some he marries one of the girls, in another he is their father and pushes the girl in the water, and in some he is bribed by the elder sister to push the girl back in the water. In at least one version (Davis, *More Traditional Ballads of Virginia,* p. 35) the miller's son figures in the action. Occasionally a ghost aids in revealing the murderer, but there are several American versions in which the murderer is not punished for the crime. There are also some texts where punishment is unnecessary because no one dies, and some variations have an almost comic tone.

A typical refrain to this ballad is the "bow down" given in the first version above. This type of refrain seems to be most common in those communities where the ballad was also used to accompany a dance. Other common refrains include the "juniper, gentian, and rosemary," nonsense lines like "sing i dum," "hey ho, my Nannie," and "bonnery-O." The "wind and rain" refrain contained in the second version below seems to be a later development and a most interesting innovation. Here, it serves not only to emphasize the plaintive nature of the song but even becomes a functional part of the story because it is the tune which the instrument plays. Here the instrument made from the dead girl's body is a more important part of the story than the cruel murder which is the focus of the first version given here.

Paul G. Brewster published an extensive study of this ballad in which he concluded that it began in Norway at some time before 1600 and spread to Scandinavia, then on to Britain and the West. Brewster, however, believes the story to be of Slavic origin. This theory refutes an earlier thesis that the ballad was originally composed in Britain and then split into two versions, one of which came to Norway and the other to Denmark. In an article in the *Journal of American Folklore,* Harbison Parker offered the idea that the ballad originated in western Scandinavia with the British versions deriving from Faroe or Norwegian texts. Whatever the real origins of the ballad, it is generally accepted that American texts usually follow the English tradition. The beaver hat, the failure to call the hair yellow, and the introductory stanza, such as in the first version given here, are all considered to be English traits.

155

Both versions given above were collected in 1962 by George Foss, the first from Mildred Creighton of Carrie, Kentucky, and the second from Dan Tate of Fancy Gap, Virginia.

Ole Banghum

COLLECTED BY MARION TAYLOR PAGE FROM NANCY MCCUDDY STEVENSON, ST.
BETHLEHEM, TENNESSEE. EXACT DATE OF COLLECTION NOT GIVEN BUT WAS
SOMETIME BETWEEN 1953 AND 1955. TRANSCRIBED BY MARION TAYLOR PAGE.

Ole Banghum, will you hunt and ride;
　　Dellum down, dellum.
Ole Banghum, will you hunt and ride
With sword and pistol by your side?
　　Corbe ki kuttle dum, kille ko qum.

There is a wild hog in these woods.
　　Dellum, down, dellum.
There is a wild hog in these woods;
He'll eat your flesh and drink your blood.
　　Corbe ki kuttle dum, kille ko qum.

Ole Banghum drew his wooden knife.
　　Dellum, down, dellum.
Ole Banghum drew his wooden knife,
And swore he'd ease him of his life.
　　Corbe ki kuttle dum, kille ko qum.

Ole Banghum blew so loud and shrill;
　　Dellum, down, dellum.
Ole Banghum blew so loud and shrill
The wild hog heard at Temple Hill.
　　Corbe ki kuttle dum, kille ko qum.

The wild hog came with such a dash;
　　Dellum, down, dellum.
The wild hog came with such a dash
He tore his way through oak and ash.
　　Corbe ki kuttle dum, kille ko qum.

They fought four hours in the day.
    Dellum, down, dellum.
They fought four hours in the day.
At length the wild hog stole away.
    Corbe ki kuttle dum, kille ko qum.

Ole Banghum went to the wild hog's den.
    Dellum, down, dellum.
Ole Banghum went to the wild hog's den,
And saw the bones of a thousand men.
    Corbe ki kuttle dum, kille ko qum.

Throughout its history this ballad has run the gamut from a serious Arthurian romance to a burlesqued backwoods melodrama. Listed as number 18 under the title "Sir Lionel" in Child's collection, the first report of this ballad is in the 1760s but it is older than that by at least a century. Apparently, the original story told of a knight who finds a lady sitting in a tree who tells him that a wild boar has slain another knight. The protagonist kills the boar, receiving several bad wounds in the process. It turns out that the boar belonged to a giant who demands that the knight forfeit his hawks and leash and the little finger of his right hand in retribution for killing the animal. The knight refuses to submit to such disgrace, but as he is gravely injured the giant allows him time for his wounds to heal on the condition that he leave his lady as security for his return. At the end of the appointed time the knight comes back sound and well and kills the giant. In America this extended story is usually reduced to little more than a fight with a boar—often, as in the present version, called a wild hog, perhaps because "hog" sounds better to American ears than "boar."

Versions of "Sir Lionel" have been reported from Maine, North Carolina, Virginia, Oklahoma, Vermont, Kentucky, New York, Missouri, West Virginia, Arkansas, and Tennessee. The "Sir Lionel" title is rarely used by American singers; instead the ballad is known as "Bangum and the Boar," "Bingham," "Brangy Well," "Jason and the Wild Boar," "Old Banghum," "Rach's Spinning Song," "The Wild Hog," "Banghum Rid by the Riverside," and "The Jobal Hunter," among other titles. Four story types are found in the United States, three of which mention the girl but focus almost entirely on the hunt for the vicious hog. None mentions the giant but one version reported from Tennessee and Oklahoma speaks of a "witch-wife" who curses the protagonist for killing her pig and demands his hawk, hound, and lady in retribution. He refuses and, after killing her, proceeds on his way. In one story type it is the King, rather than a knight, who is the hero, and he fights the boar in his den but is killed himself. In another story type Bangum and the maid marry but only after he kills the boar.

The present version was collected sometime between 1953 and 1955 (the exact date is not given) by Marion Taylor Page from Nancy McCuddy Stevenson, St. Bethlehem, Tennessee. For more information about Page and Stevenson see the notes to "Lord Lovel" in Volume I. As the first verse here indicates, some versions of "Sir Lionel" have been influenced by "Frog Went a-Courting."

Sentimental Songs of Death and Dying

Daisy Deane

ORIGINAL MELODY LINE OF "DAISY DEANE" WITH WORDS AND MUSIC MOSTLY BY LIEUT. T.F. WINTHROP AND JAMES R. MURRAY OF THE MASSACHUSETTS VOLUNTEERS. PUBLISHED BY ROOT AND CADY, CHICAGO.

Lyrics published in 1863

'Twas down in the meadows, the violets were blowing,
And the springtime grass was fresh and green;
And the birds by the brooklet their sweet songs were singing
When I first met my darling Daisy Deane.

CHORUS:

None knew thee but to love thee, thou dear one of my heart,
O thy mem'ry is ever fresh and green,
Tho' the sweet buds may wither and fond hearts be broken,
Still I'll love thee my darling Daisy Deane.

Her eye soft and tender, the violets outvieing,
And a fairer form was never seen—
With her brown silken tresses, her cheek like the roses,
There was none like my darling Daisy Deane.

CHORUS: (same as before)

162

The bright flowers are faded, the young grass has fallen,
And a dark cloud hovers o'er the scene:
For the death angel took her, and left me in sorrow
For my lost one, my darling Daisy Deane.

CHORUS: (same as before)

O, down in the meadows I still love to wander,
Where the young grass grew so fresh and green;
But the bright golden visions of springtime have faded
With the flowers, and my darling Daisy Deane.

CHORUS: (same as before)

Daisy Deane

COLLECTED BY KAY L. COTHRAN FROM GEORGE W. MITCHELL, THOMASTON, GEORGIA, DECEMBER 28, 1967. TRANSCRIBED BY KAY L. COTHRAN.

'Twas down in the meadow, the violets were blooming,
And th' springtime grass was fresh an' green.
An' th' birds by th' brooklet their sweet songs were singing,
When I first met m' darling Daisy Deane.

CHORUS:

None knew thee but to love thee, thou dear one of my heart.
Oh the mem'ry is ever fresh an' green.
Though th' sweet buds ma' wither, and fond hearts be broken,
There is none like my darling Daisy Deane.

Her eyes soft an' tender, the violets outvying
And a fairer form was never seen,
Her brown silken tresses, her cheeks like the roses,
There was none like my darling Daisy Deane.

CHORUS: (same as before)

This ballad from the Civil War era was written by Lieutenant T.F. Winthrop and James R. Murray and was probably first published in 1863. Evidently it had a measure of popularity, for the song was issued in at least two sheet music editions and on a broadside that was sold in Boston. Most likely the earliest sheet music publication was by Root &

Cady of Chicago but it was also published by S. Brainard's Sons in Cleveland. Because the Winthrop and Murray original is rarely seen today it is given here. The song, of course, also made it into oral tradition and, although rarely found in folksong collections, was probably fairly commonly known at one time. Kentucky-born entertainer Louis Marshall "Grandpa" Jones learned it from his mother who claimed it was based on a true event (See Louis M. Jones and Charles K. Wolfe, *Everybody's Grandpa: Fifty Years Behind the Mike* [Knoxville: University of Tennessee Press, 1984], p. 28). Jones refers to the song as a murder ballad (Jones and Wolfe, p. 116) although nothing in the present text suggests that this is a murder story.

The present version was collected by Kay L. Cothran from George W. Mitchell in Thomaston, Georgia, December 28, 1967. At the time of this collection, Mr. Mitchell, a former country schoolteacher, was ninety-six years old and, although rather hard of hearing, was apparently an enthusiastic informant. He provided Cothran considerable information about traditions of his youth, particularly about children's singing games and ballads and non-narrative folksongs. Mitchell also gave much detail about various traditional practices such as log construction, soap making, and hominy boiling, and offered his reflections on changing times. Mr. Mitchell said he learned "Daisy Deane" from his mother who sang it "away back over a hundred years ago," a time period that is not outside the realm of possibility for at the time he made that remark the ballad was at least 104 years old.

Kitty Wells

COLLECTED BY DIANNE DUGAW FROM LAWRENCE HIGHTOWER, CANAAN MOUNTAIN, ARKANSAS, AUGUST 1973. TRANSCRIBED BY DIANNE DUGAW.

Dear friends, you ask me why I weep,
And why like others I'm not gay,
And why the tears roll down my cheek,
From early morn 'til close of day.

Dear friends, my story you all may hear,
For in my memory fresh it dwells,
I've thought through all the troubled years
On the grave of my sweet Kitty Wells.

REFRAIN:

When the morning birds were singing in the morning,
And the myrtle and the ivy were in bloom,
Oh the sun on the hilltop were a-dawning,
It was there we laid her in the tomb.

I never shall forget that day,
That we together in the dell,
I kissed her cheek and named the day
That I would marry Kitty Wells.
Oh, death came in my cabin door,
And stole from me my dear, my bride.
And when I saw she was no more,
I laid my banjo down and cried.

REFRAIN:

Now springtime has no charms for me
(Though flowers are blooming in the dell)
I love her more (than I can tell)
(As I think of) my sweet Kitty Wells.
Then (shall I still recall that day)
That we together in the dell,
There's one sweet face I do not see,
The face of my sweet Kitty Wells.

There is some dispute about who is the lyricist and composer of this piece. The earliest known publication, in 1858, credited both words and music to Charles E. Atherton, but in 1861 the same publisher, Stephen T. Gordon of New York, issued "the only correct and authorized edition," which was credited to T. Brigham Bishop. One year earlier, in 1860, a penny song sheet of the ballad was issued with authorship ascribed to Thomas Sloan, Jr. Of these three men, only Bishop seems to have been very active as a popular songwriter. His "Leaf by Leaf the Roses Fall" (1865) and "My Poor Heart Is Sad With its Dreaming" (1870) were among his productions; neither, of course, can be given anything but the most minor status in popular song history. Yet despite Bishop's other pop song activity and Atherton's prior claim, most commentators on this ballad have accepted Sloan as the lyricist-composer. Actually, it is entirely possible that none of the three was responsible for the song. That the publisher took pains to note on the 1861 edition that this was the "only correct and authorized" version suggests that there may have been many more published editions of the song than are now known. In nineteenth-century America, copyright laws were less rigidly enforced than they are now and "pilfering" other people's songs was not uncommon. But if one must go on the basis of evidence in hand, then the song must be ascribed to Atherton and dates back to 1858. It is known that the song was popular with minstrel show singers of the Civil War era.

One fact about "Kitty Wells" is very clear, namely that it had the power to persist in tradition. To date, it has been reported from Michigan, West Virginia, North Carolina, Texas, Kentucky, and Arkansas and is probably more widely known than this list indicates. Because of its known origins in the commercial music industry, "Kitty Wells" is among the category of songs that many collectors, particularly those active before 1950, simply did not bother to report. Certainly, the song's popularity with commercial country entertainers aided its popularity with traditional singers. Particularly important are the 78s by two of the most successful country performers of the 1920s, Vernon Dalhart and Bradley Kincaid. The ballad was frequently reprinted in country song

167

folios of the 1920s and 1930s.

The version given here was collected in August 1973 by Diane Dugaw from the singing of Lawrence Hightower of Bee Branch, Arkansas. Hightower, who was sixty-nine years old at the time this recording was made, grew up on Canaan Mountain about ten miles southwest of Marshall, Arkansas. His repertoire, which consists largely of sentimental songs about death and love, such as "Kitty Wells," was learned primarily from an older sister, Effy Hightower Harris, and from "old friends a way back yonder." Lawrence did not indicate the exact source of his version of "Kitty Wells" which he sang to the accompaniment of his own guitar and his nephew's electric guitar.

The Letter Edged in Black

RECORDED IN JULY 1984 BY AN UNIDENTIFIED FIELDWORKER FROM LOUISE SANDERS, PERRY, FLORIDA. TRANSCRIPTION BY DREW BEISSWENGER.

I was standing by my window yesterday morning
A-looking wide of worry or of care,
When I saw the postman coming up the pathway
With such a happy look and jolly air.

He rang the bell and he whistled as he waited,
Then he said, "Good morning to you, Jack."
But he little knew the sorrow that he brought me
When he handed me that letter edged in black.

With trembling hands I took this letter from him,
I broke the seal and this is what it said,
Come home, my boy, your dear old father wants you,
Come home, my boy, your dear old mother's dead.

I bowed my head in silence and in sorrow,
The sunshine of my life it all has fled
Since the postman brought that letter yesterday morning,
Saying come home, my boy, your dear old mother's dead.

Those angry words I wish I'd never spoke them,
You know I did not mean them don't you, Jack?
My eyes are dim my poor old heart is breaking
As I'm writing you this letter edged in black.

This widely-known ballad was written by a Kansas City resident who spent a very brief time as a songwriter. Hattie Hicks Woodbury (1862–1953) had only a three-year career as a popular lyricist from 1896 to 1899, which nicely coincided with the tenure of her husband, Frank H. Woodbury, as president of the Kansas City (Missouri) Talking Machine Company. This connection is important because his company published several of her efforts, including two Spanish-American War songs, "My Father Was a Sailor on the *Maine*" and " 'Remember the *Maine*' Will

Be Our War Cry." Musically illiterate, Mrs. Woodbury had her songs set in notation by Kansas City ragtime composer Charles L. Johnson (1876–1950), who performed for twenty years as a pianist in local orchestras, hotels, and theaters. Johnson, best known for his 1906 composition "Dill Pickles Rag," also wrote several pop songs. In 1897, when he was only twenty-one, he notated Mrs. Woodbury's biggest hit, "The Letter Edged in Black." For this, and all of her other compositions, she used the pseudonym of Hattie Nevada. The source of her alias is unknown as is her reason for its use. Possibly she employed it in deference to her husband, who, as is already noted, was her publisher, thereby attempting to stave off any feelings of impropriety. Or perhaps she used the pseudonym simply because it wasn't considered proper for fashionable matrons of the day to write popular songs, and in this way she could disguise her identity. It is also possible that Mrs. Woodbury merely thought that adopting a pseudonym was the thing to do if one was a writer. At this point in time it is unlikely that anyone will discover the motivation behind the use of an alias. But, regardless of the name used, it is certain that "The Letter Edged in Black" was very successful.

Woodbury's song was one of the first ballads recorded by a country performer. In 1924 Fiddlin' John Carson (1868–1949) did the number for Okeh Records in a rather archaic style of singing. This version was followed in subsequent years by renditions from Marion Try Slaughter (1883–1948), who is better known as Vernon Dalhart, and Bradley Kincaid (1895–), among others. Probably the rather frequent appearance of the ballad on commercial recordings made it even less palatable to folksong collectors. Cecil Sharp, working in the southern Appalachians from 1916 to 1918, sneeringly dismissed it and most later collectors followed suit. Vance Randolph, who spent most of his adult life collecting various kinds of folklore in the Ozarks, was an exception to this general rule. He recognized that even though a song might not be traditional it was still important to document it as part of a folksinger's repertoire. The first version Randolph noted was a text given him in 1934 by Lucille Morris of Springfield, Missouri, who had it from a Mrs. Minnie Ferguson, also of Springfield. Seven years later, on September 21, 1941, he recorded a version from a Mr. Tommy Davis of Galena, Missouri. Evidently either the latter text was learned from oral tradition or the singer had partially forgotten it, for it consists of only four four-line verses rather than the usual three eight-line verses and four-line chorus.

Just when the practice of notifying kin of the death of a family member using an envelope bearing a distinctive black around the outside edge started is unknown, but it may have been as early as the 1830s. It was relatively common by the 1860s and still widely practiced in the United States as late as the 1920s. By World War II it seems to have fallen into disuse, although even as late as the 1960s it was occasionally found. For example, in the late 1960s an auto parts firm sent out to its customers in Oklahoma a black-bordered card telling of the death of the company's president. As recently as the 1970s the practice was still common in Holland but it seems to be a thing of the past in the United States.

The version of "The Letter Edged in Black" given here was collected by an unidentified fieldworker for the Florida Folklife Programs from Louise Sanders of Perry, Florida. The ballad was recorded in July 1984, at which time Sanders was seventy-two years old. She learned this, and other songs in her repertoire, as a girl growing up in the southern Georgia town of Moultrie. She often sang with family and friends on the front porch or in the parlor where a pump organ was used for accompaniment. Sanders has lived in a number of north Florida communities in the last fifty years but for the past several years has resided in Perry.

Little Bessie

COLLECTED BY GEORGE FOSS FROM VIOLA COLE, FANCY GAP, VIRGINIA, 1962.
TRANSCRIBED BY GEORGE FOSS.

Hug me closer, mother, closer;
Put your arms around me tight.
For I'm cold and tired mother
And I feel so strange tonight.

Something hurts me here, dear mother,
Like a stone upon my breast
And I wonder, wonder, mother,
Why it is I cannot rest.

All the day while you were working
As I lay upon my bed,
I was trying to be patient
And to think of what you said.

Just before the lamps were lighted,
Just before the children came,
When my room was very quiet,
I heard someone call my name.

"Come up here, my little Bessie,
Come up here and live with me,
Where no children ever suffer
Through a long eternity."

An' I wondered, wondered, mother,
Who so sweet upon me smiled,
An' I knew it must be Jesus
When he whispered, "Come, my child."

An' I wondered, wondered, mother,
Who had called and I must go.
Go to sleep no more to suffer,
Mother don't be crying so.

There were little children singing,
Sweetest songs I ever heard.
They were sweeter, mother, sweeter,
Than the sweetest singing bird.

Way up yonder in the portals
That is shining very fair,
Little Bessie now is sheltered
By the Savior's love and care.

This mournful tale from nineteenth-century America is quite popular with country and bluegrass recording artists and with traditional singers but is rarely found in folksong and ballad collections. Despite its popularity and its several recordings, little of its history is known; the lyricist-composer is anonymous, and even original date of publication is unknown. It is generally thought to date from the 1860s, primarily because it is found in several songsters of that decade. Unfortunately, no author is given for these texts. A song titled "Little Bessie," published by S. Brainard & Sons, Cleveland, and attributed to someone named Keutchman, was available in 1870. Possibly this is the same song but, unfortunately, this sheet music apparently no longer exists. All versions on commercial recordings and those from field collections share essentially the same melody, usually an indication that a ballad has not strayed far from its printed original.

The present version was collected by George Foss in 1962 from Viola Cole, Fancy Gap, Virginia. Unfortunately, no details are given concerning Cole or the recording session.

The Old Elm Tree

COLLECTED MAY 1980 BY W.K. MCNEIL FROM FLOYD M. HOLLAND, MOUNTAIN VIEW, ARKANSAS. TRANSCRIPTION BY DREW BEISSWENGER.

There's a path by the lone deserted mill,
And the stream by the old bridge, broken still,
And the willow boughs are bending low
To the green, mossy bank where the violets grow.
The wild birds are singing the same sweet lay
That stirred me in the dear old days
When Lora, my beautiful, sat with me
On the mossy green seat 'neath the old elm tree.

It was there with the bright blue skies above
I told her the tale of my heart's true love.
And there ere the blossoms of summer died
She whispered the promise to be my bride.
And here fell the tears of our parting sore.
Oh, little we dreamed that we'd meet no more,
And that ere I came from the far blue sea
They would make her grave 'neath the old elm tree.

Cruel and false were the tales they told
That my vows were false and my old love cold,
That my tyrant heart held another dear,
While I made the vows that was whispered here.
Then her cheeks grew pale with the crushed heart pain
And her beautiful lips never smiled again.
And she bitterly wept where none could see,
She wept for the past, 'neath the old elm tree.
She died and they parted her sunny hair
O'er the cold pale brow death had left so fair.
And they laid her to rest, where the sweet young flowers
Would watch by her side through the long summer hours.

Oh, Lora, dear Lora, my heart's last love,
Shall we meet in the angel's home above?
There's nothing on earth so dear to me
As thy lonely grave 'neath the old elm tree.

Joseph Philbrick Webster (1819–1875), a native of Manchester, New Hampshire, who also lived in most of the other states that existed during his lifetime, is generally forgotten today but several of his compositions are well remembered. The first of these is "Lorena" (1857) which became one of the most popular songs of the Civil War—strangely a bigger hit in the South than the North, even though J.P. Webster and lyricist Henry De LaFayette Webster (no relation) were strong anti-slavery advocates. It is still loved, as is affirmed by numerous recordings, arrangements, and its use in the scores of a large number of western films, the most notable being John Ford's *The Searchers* (1956).

In 1860 Webster and lyricist Maud Irving produced "I'll Twine 'mid the Ringlets," a number destined to be more popular in the twentieth century than in its own day. Thanks primarily to a 1928 recording by the Carter Family this song is now known as "Wildwood Flower." The Carters must also share the blame for the garbling of the lyrics that makes much of Webster and Irving's tale of unrequited love virtually unintelligible. Actually, though, the melody is better known today than the words.

Eight years later, in 1868, Webster and his most frequent lyricist, S. Fillmore Bennett, wrote "In the Sweet By and By," one of the best-known hymns in the English language. Among Webster's other hits are such now forgotten classics as "Softly, Lightly, Sweetly Sing" (1853), a great success for the Blakeley Family, a popular singing group of the day; "Little Maud" (1859), a musical adaptation of a Thomas Bailey Aldrich poem; and "Brave Men, Behold Your Fallen Chief" (1862), a tribute to a Civil War hero, Elmer Ellsworth (1837–1861). A prolific writer, Webster is said to have produced over one thousand compositions during his relatively brief lifetime. In addition, he was known as a virtuoso on the flute, violin, and piano. He was among the few popular songwriters of the nineteenth century who was trained in music, having studied under the famous Lowell Mason in Boston.

On "The Old Elm Tree" Webster collaborated with Sarah S. Bolton, a sometime pop song lyricist of the day. The song they wrote had a limited success in its day but has lived on in the memories of traditional singers. It has been reported as a folk ballad from Kansas, Missouri, Minnesota, and Nebraska, although it is better known in tradition than that statistic indicates. The version given here is from the singing of Floyd Maurice Holland (1891–1986) of Mountain View, Arkansas. For many years Holland was a favorite performer at the Arkansas Folk Festival held annually in Mountain View. Although he was best known for singing a comic song called "Susie Lick the Ladle," his personal favorite was "The Old Elm Tree." Holland learned the song sometime around the turn of the century from members of his family. He recalled hearing that a cousin who went to Illinois in 1879 returned with the song, which had been written in 1871 by Joseph Philbrick Webster.

Orphan Girl

COLLECTED BY KAY L. COTHRAN FROM GEORGE W. MITCHELL, THOMASTON, GEORGIA,
DECEMBER 28, 1967. TRANSCRIBED BY KAY L. COTHRAN.

"No home, no home," pled an orphan girl,
At th' door of a palace hall,
As she trembling stood on the polished step,
And leaned on th' marble wall.

Her dress was torn and her feet were bare,
And snow had covered her head.
"Oh give me a home," she feebly cried,
"A home and a piece of bread."

"My father alas I never knew,"
An' th' tears filled her eyes so bright.
"My mother sleeps in a new made grave.
'Tis an orphan begs tonight."

The rich man dressed in 'is velvet robes,
An' stood in th' parlor door,
His cruel lips with scorn as 'e said,
"No room, no bread for th' poor."

"I must perish," she said as she sank on th' steps,
An' tried to cover her feet
With the tattered dress all covered with snow,
Yes, covered with snow and sleet.

Th' rich man lay on 'is velvet couch,
An' dreamed of 'is silver an' gold,
While the orphan lay on a bed of snow,
An' murmured, "So cold, so cold."

Th' morning dawned an' the orphan girl
Still lay at the rich man's door,
But 'er soul had fled to that home above,
Where there's bread an' home for th' poor.

This ballad appears in the Cooper edition of the *Sacred Harp* with the tune credited to "Eld. C.G. Keith, Nov. 1, 1906" but, according to Henry Belden, George Pullen Jackson thought the ascription merely indicated the source of the copy rather than composition. Whatever the case, the tune owes a great deal to "The Braes o' Balquidder" or "Balquither," a song popular in America in the 1820s. To date, the lyrics have not been attributed to anyone but stylistically they are akin to popular poetry and songs from 1830 to 1900 and probably originated during those decades. There is little variation between versions, even in titles, suggesting that the ballad is not far removed from its printed origins. Except for an Iowa text and one from Missouri, all versions collected from traditional singers have been reported from the South.

The present version was collected December 28, 1967, by Kay L. Cothran from George W. Mitchell, Thomaston, Georgia. For more information about Cothran and Mitchell see the notes for "Daisy Deane."

Notes

Biblio-Discography

This biblio-discography is arranged in four sections: A. Basic references, B. Other references, C. 78 rpm records, and D. LP recordings. Section A consists of those books often cited in these notes, each volume being coded by a keyword. Usually a partial or complete (generally the latter) text appears on the pages cited. A full listing of these publications is given following these prefatory remarks; they are preceded by their keyword. Section B consists of printed references not in section A; these may be studies of individual songs or collections. Section C includes 78 albums as well as individual records, and section D includes both new releases and reissues of 78 rpm records. None of the sections should be construed as exhaustive lists of either publications or records dealing with an individual song. Instead, they are merely intended as a representative sampling of what is available; in most cases the listed items could be greatly increased. Where nothing appears under a numbered section, I was unable to locate any relevant items in that category for the specific song.

Basic References

Abrahams & Foss	Abrahams, Roger D. and George Foss. *Anglo-American Folksong Style*. Englewood Cliffs, New Jersey: Prentice-Hall, Inc., 1968.
Abrahams & Riddle	Abrahams, Roger D. *A Singer and Her Songs: Almeda Riddle's Book of Ballads*. Baton Rouge: Louisiana State University Press, 1970.
Allen	Allen, Jules Verne. *Cowboy Lore*. San Antonio: The Naylor Printing Co., 1933.
Arnold	Arnold, Byron. *Folksongs of Alabama*. University: University of Alabama Press, 1950.
Barry	Barry, Phillips, Fannie Hardy Eckstorm, and Mary W. Smyth. *British Ballads from Maine*. New Haven: Yale University Press, 1929.
Belden	Belden, Henry M. *Ballads and Songs Collected by the Missouri Folk-Lore Society*. 1940. 2nd ed. Columbia: University of Missouri Press, 1955.
Boette	Boette, Marie. *Singa Hipsy Doodle and Other Folk Songs of West Virginia*. Parsons, West Virginia: McClain Printing Co., 1971.

Botkin	Botkin, Benjamin A. *A Treasury of American Folklore: Stories, Ballads, and Traditions of the People.* New York: Crown Publishers, 1944.
Botkin (1949)	Botkin, Benjamin A. *A Treasury of Southern Folklore.* New York: Crown Publishers, 1949.
Brewster	Brewster, Paul G. *Ballads and Songs of Indiana.* 1940. New York: Folklorica, 1981.
Bronson	Bronson, Bertrand H. *The Singing Tradition of Child's Popular Ballads.* Princeton: Princeton University Press, 1976.
Brown II	*The Frank C. Brown Collection of North Carolina Folklore. Volume 2. Folk Ballads.* Edited by Henry M. Belden and Arthur Palmer Hudson. Durham: Duke University Press, 1952.
Brown IV	*The Frank C. Brown Collection of North Carolina Folklore. Volume 4. The Music of the Ballads.* Edited by Jan Philip Schinhan. Durham: Duke University Press, 1962.
Browne	Browne, Ray B. *The Alabama Folk Lyric: A Study in Origins and Media of Dissemination.* Bowling Green, Ohio: Bowling Green University Popular Press, 1979.
Burt	Burt, Olive Woolley. *American Murder Ballads and Their Stories.* New York: Oxford University Press, 1958.
Burton & Manning I	Burton, Thomas G. and Ambrose N. Manning. *East Tennessee State University Collection of Folklore: Folksongs.* Johnson City: East Tennessee State University, 1967.
Burton & Manning II	Burton, Thomas G. and Ambrose N. Manning. *East Tennessee State University Collection of Folklore. Volume 2. Folksongs.* Johnson City: East Tennessee State University, 1969.
Bush I	Bush, Michael E. *Folk Songs of Central West Virginia.* Ravenswood, West Virginia: Custom Printing, 1969.
Bush II	Bush, Michael E. *Folk Songs of Central West Virginia.* Ravenswood, West Virginia: Custom Printing, 1970.
Cambiaire	Cambiaire, Celestin Pierre. *East Tennessee and Western Virginia Mountain Ballads.* London: The Mitre Press, 1934.
Carey	Carey, George G. *Maryland Folk Legends and Folk Songs.* Cambridge, Maryland: Tidewater Publishers, 1971.
Cazden	Cazden, Norman. *The Abelard Folksong Book.* New York: Abelard-Schuman, 1958.
Chappell	Chappell, Louis W. *Folk-Songs of Roanoke and the Albemarle.* Morgantown, West Virginia: Ballad Press, 1939.
Chase	Chase, Richard. *American Folk Tales and Songs.* New York: The New American Library of World Literature, Inc., 1956.
Cohen & Seeger	Cohen, John and Mike Seeger. *The New Lost City Ramblers Song Book.* New York: Oak Publications, 1964.
Cohen, N.	Cohen, Norm. *Long Steel Rail: The Railroad in American Folksong.* Urbana: University of Illinois Press, 1981.
Combs & Wilgus	Combs, Josiah H. *Folk-Songs of the Southern United States.* Edited by D. K. Wilgus. Austin: University of Texas Press, 1967.
Cox	Cox, John Harrington. *Folk-Songs of the South.* 1925. Reprint, New York: Dover Publications, Inc., 1967.

Creighton (1971)　　　　Creighton, Helen. *Folksongs from Southern New Brunswick.* Ottawa: National Museum of Canada, 1971.

Creighton (1962)　　　　Creighton, Helen. *Maritime Folk Songs.* Toronto: Ryerson Press, 1962.

Creighton & Senior　　　Creighton, Helen and Doreen H. Senior. *Traditional Songs from Nova Scotia.* Toronto: Ryerson Press, 1950.

Cutting　　　　　　　　Cutting, Edith. *Lore of an Adirondack County.* Ithaca, New York: Cornell University Press, 1943.

Davis (1929)　　　　　　Davis, Arthur Kyle, Jr. *Traditional Ballads of Virginia.* Cambridge: Harvard University Press, 1929.

Davis (1949)　　　　　　_____ . *Folk Songs of Virginia: A Descriptive Index and Classification.* Durham: Duke University Press, 1949.

Davis (1960)　　　　　　_____ . *More Traditional Ballads of Virginia: Collected with the Cooperation of Members of the Virginia Folklore Society.* Chapel Hill: University of North Carolina Press, 1960.

Dean　　　　　　　　　Dean, Michael C. *The Flying Cloud and One Hundred and Fifty Other Old Time Songs and Ballads.* Virginia, Minnesota: The Quickprint, 1922.

Downes & Siegmeister　　Downes, Olin and Elie Siegmeister. *A Treasury of American Song.* New York: Alfred A. Knopf, Inc., 1943.

Eddy　　　　　　　　　Eddy, Mary Olive. *Ballads and Songs From Ohio.* 1939. Reprint, Hatboro, Pennsylvania: Folklore Associates, 1964.

Emrich (1972)　　　　　Emrich, Duncan. *Folklore on the American Land.* Boston: Little, Brown and Company, 1972.

Emrich (1974)　　　　　_____ . *American Folk Poetry: An Anthology.* Boston: Little, Brown and Company, 1974.

Fauset　　　　　　　　Fauset, Arthur Huff. *Folklore from Nova Scotia.* New York: American Folklore Society, 1931.

Fife & Fife　　　　　　Fife, Austin E. and Alta S. Fife. *Cowboy and Western Songs.* New York: Clarkson N. Potter, 1969.

Finger　　　　　　　　Finger, Charles J. *Frontier Ballads.* Garden City, New York: Doubleday, Page, 1927.

Flanders　　　　　　　Flanders, Helen Hartness. *Ancient Ballads Traditionally Sung in New England.* Philadelphia: University of Pennsylvania Press, 1960. 4 volumes.

Flanders & Olney　　　　_____ , and Marguerite Olney. *Ballads Migrant in New England.* New York: Farrar, Straus, and Young, 1953.

Fowke　　　　　　　　Fowke, Edith. *Traditional Singers and Songs From Ontario.* Hatboro, Pennsylvania: Folklore Associates, 1965.

Fowke & Johnston　　　_____ , and Richard Johnston. *More Folk Songs of Canada.* Waterloo, Ontario: Waterloo Music Company, 1967.

Fuson　　　　　　　　Fuson, Henry H. *Ballads of the Kentucky Highlands.* London: The Mitre Press, 1931.

Gainer　　　　　　　　Gainer, Patrick. *Folk Songs from the West Virginia Hills.* Grantsville, West Virginia: Seneca Books, 1975.

Gardner & Chickering　　Gardner, Emelyn E. and Geraldine Jencks Chickering. *Ballads and Songs of Southern Michigan.* 1939. Reprint, Hatboro, Pennsylvania: Folklore Associates, 1967.

Greenleaf & Mansfield　　Greenleaf, Elisabeth Bristol and Grace Yarrow Mansfield. *Ballads and Sea Songs of Newfoundland.* Cambridge: Harvard University Press, 1933.

Grover   Grover, Carrie B. *A Heritage of Songs.* Edited by Anne L. Griggs. Norwood, Pennsylvania: Norwood Editions, n. d.

Heart   *Heart Songs Dear to the American People.* New York: World Syndicate Company, 1909.

Henry (1934)   Henry, Mellinger E. *Songs Sung in the Southern Appalachians.* London: The Mitre Press, 1934.

Henry (1938)   _____ . *Folk-Songs from the Southern Highlands.* New York: J. J. Augustin, 1938.

Henry & Matteson   _____ , and Maurice Matteson. *Twenty-nine Beech Mountain Folk Songs and Ballads.* New York: G. Schirmer, 1936.

High   High, Fred. *Old, Old Folk Songs.* Berryville, Arkansas: no publisher or date of publication given.

Hubbard   Hubbard, Lester A. *Ballads and Songs from Utah.* Salt Lake City: University of Utah Press, 1961.

Hudson   Hudson, Arthur Palmer. *Folk-Songs of Mississippi and Their Background.* 1936. Reprint, New York: Folklorica, 1981.

Ives   Ives, Burl. *The Burl Ives Song Book: American Song in Historical Perspective.* New York: Ballantine Books, 1963.

Jameson   Jameson, Gladys V. *Sweet Rivers of Song: Authentic Ballads Hymns, Folksongs from the Appalachian Region.* Berea, Kentucky: Berea College, 1967.

Jekyll   Jekyll, Walter. *Jamaican Song and Story: Annancy Stories. Digging Sings, Ring Tunes, and Dancing Tunes.* 1907. Reprint, New York: Dover Publications, Inc., 1966.

Jones (1980)   Jones, Loyal. *Radio's 'Kentucky Mountain Boy' Bradley Kincaid.* Berea, Kentucky; Berea College Appalachian Center, 1980.

Jones (1984)   _____ . *Minstrel of the Appalachians: The Story of Bascom Lamar Lunsford.* Boone, North Carolina: Appalachian Consortium Press, 1984.

Joyner   Joyner, Charles W. *Folk Song in South Carolina.* Columbia: University of South Carolina Press, 1971.

Kennedy   Kennedy, Charles O'Brien. *American Ballads: Folk Treasures of the American Past in Verse and Song.* Greenwich, Connecticut: Fawcett Publications, Inc., 1952.

Killion & Waller   Killian, Ronald G. and Charles T. Waller. *A Treasury of Georgia Folklore.* Atlanta: Cherokee Publishing Company, 1972.

Larkin   Larkin, Margaret. *Singing Cowboy.* 1931. Reprint, New York: Oak Publications, 1963.

Leach   Leach, MacEdward. *The Ballad Book.* 1955. Reprint, New York; A. S. Barnes & Company, Inc., n. d.

Leisy   Leisy, James F. *The Folk Song Abecedary.* New York: Bonanza Books, 1966.

Lingenfelter   Lingenfelter, Richard E., Richard A. Dwyer, and David Cohen. *Songs of the American West.* Berkeley: University of California Press, 1968.

Linscott   Linscott, Eloise Hubbard. *Folk Songs of Old New England.* New York: Macmillan, 1939.

Lomax, A.   Lomax, Alan. *The Folk Songs of North America.* Garden City, New York: Doubleday, 1960.

Lomax, J.   Lomax, John A. *Adventures of a Ballad Hunter.* New York: Macmillan, 1947.

Lomax & Lomax   Lomax, John A. and Alan Lomax. *Cowboy Songs and Other Frontier Ballads.* Revised edition. New York: Macmillan, 1938.

MacColl & Seeger   MacColl, Ewan and Peggy Seeger. *Travellers' Songs From England and Scotland.* Knoxville: The University of Tennessee Press, 1977.

MacIntosh   MacIntosh, David S. *Folk Songs and Singing Games of the Illinois Ozarks.* Edited by Dale R. Whiteside. Carbondale: Southern Illinois University Press, 1974.

MacKenzie (1919)   MacKenzie, W. Roy. *The Quest of the Ballad.* Princeton, New Jersey: Princeton University Press, 1919.

MacKenzie (1928)   _____ . *Ballads and Sea Songs from Nova Scotia.* 1928. Reprint, Hatboro, Pennsylvania: Folklore Associates, 1963.

McGill   McGill, Josephine. *Folk-Songs of the Kentucky Mountains.* New York: Boosey, 1917.

Manny & Wilson   Manny, Louise and James Reginald Wilson. *Songs of Miramichi.* Fredericton, New Brunswick: Brunswick Press, 1968.

Moore & Moore   Moore, Ethel and Chauncy O. Moore. *Ballads and Folk Songs of the Southwest.* Norman: University of Oklahoma Press, 1964.

Morris   Morris, Alton C. *Folksongs of Florida.* 1950. Reprint, New York: Folklorica, 1981.

Munch   Munch, Peter A. *The Song Tradition of Tristan da Cunha.* Bloomington: Indiana University Research Center for the Language Sciences, 1970.

Neely   Neely, Charles. *Tales and Songs of Southern Illinois.* Edited by John W. Spargo. Menasha, Wisconsin: George Banta Publishing, 1938.

Niles I   Niles, John Jacob. *The Anglo-American Ballad Study Book.* New York: G. Schirmer, n. d.

Niles II   _____ . *More Songs of the Hill Folk.* New York: G. Schirmer, 1936.

Ohrlin   Ohrlin, Glenn. *The Hell-Bound Train: A Cowboy Songbook.* Urbana: University of Illinois Press, 1973.

Ord   Ord, John. *The Bothy Songs and Ballads of Aberdeen, Banff & Moray, Angus and the Mearns.* Paisley, Scotland: A. Gardner, 1930.

Owens (1950)   Owens, William A. *Texas Folk Songs.* Dallas: Southern Methodist University Press, 1950.

Owens (1983)   _____ . *Tell Me a Story, Sing Me a Song: A Texas Chronicle.* Austin: University of Texas Press, 1983.

Palmer   Palmer, Roy. *Everyman's Book of British Ballads.* London: J. M. Dent & Sons Ltd., 1980.

Parler   Parler, Mary Celestia. *An Arkansas Ballet Book.* Norwood, Pennsylvania: Norwood Editions, 1975.

Parsons (1918)   Parsons, Elsie Clews. *Folk Tales of the Andros Islands.* New York: American Folklore Society, 1918.

Parsons (1923)   _____ . *Folklore of the Sea Islands.* New York: American Folklore Society, 1923.

Peacock   Peacock, Kenneth. *Songs of the Newfoundland Outports.* 3 volumes. Ottawa: National Museum of Canada, 1965.

Peters   Peters, Harry B. *Folk Songs Out of Wisconsin.* Madison: State Historical Society of Wisconsin, 1977.

Pound   Pound, Louise. *American Ballads and Songs.* 1922. Reprint, New York: Charles Scribner's Sons, 1972.

Raim & Dunson   Raim, Ethel and Josh Dunson. *Grass Roots Harmony.* New York: Oak Publications, 1968.

Raine   Raine, James Watt. *The Land of Saddle-bags.* New York: Council of Women for Home Missions and Missionary Education Movement of the United States and Canada, 1924.

Rainey   Rainey, Leo. *Songs of the Ozark Folk.* 2nd edition. Branson, Missouri: The Ozarks Mountaineer, 1976.

Randolph I   Randolph, Vance. *The Ozarks: An American Survival of Primitive Society.* New York: Vanguard Press, 1931.

Randolph II   _____ . *Ozark Mountain Folks.* New York: Vanguard Press, 1932.

Randolph III   _____ . *Ozark Folksongs.* 1946–1950. Reprint, Columbia: University of Missouri Press, 1980. 4 volumes.

Randolph & Cohen   _____ , and Norm Cohen. *Ozark Folksongs.* 1 volume abridgement. Urbana: University of Illinois Press, 1982.

Rayburn   Rayburn, Otto Ernest. *Ozark Country.* New York: Duell, Sloan & Pearce, 1941.

Ritchie (1955)   Ritchie, Jean. *Singing Family of the Cumberlands.* 1955. Reprint, New York: Oak Publications, 1963.

Ritchie (1965)   _____ . *Folk Songs of the Southern Appalachians as Sung by Jean Ritchie.* New York: Oak Publications, 1965.

Roberts (1974)   Roberts, Leonard. *Sang Branch Settlers: Folksongs and Tales of a Kentucky Mountain Family.* Austin: University of Texas Press, 1974.

Roberts (1978)   _____ . *In the Pine: Selected Kentucky Folksongs.* Pikeville, Kentucky: Pikeville College Press, 1978.

Rosenberg   Rosenberg, Bruce A. *The Folksongs of Virginia: A Checklist of the WPA Holdings, Alderman Library. University of Virginia.* Charlottesville: University of Virginia Press, 1969.

Sandburg   Sandburg, Carl. *The American Songbag.* New York: Harcourt, Brace, 1927.

Scarborough (1925)   Scarborough, Dorothy. *On the Trail of Negro Folk-Songs.* 1925. Reprint, Hatboro, Pennsylvania: Folklore Associates, 1963.

Scarborough (1937)   _____ . *A Song Catcher in Southern Mountains: American Folk Songs of British Ancestry.* New York: Columbia University Press, 1937.

Scott   Scott, John Anthony. *The Ballad of America: The History of the United States in Song and Story.* New York: Bantam Books, Inc., 1966.

Seeger   Seeger, Pete. *American Favorite Ballads.* New York: Oak Publications, 1961.

Sharp   Sharp, Cecil J. and Maud Karpeles. *English Folk-Songs from the Southern Appalachians.* 2 volumes. London: Oxford University Press, 1932.

Shellans   Shellans, Herbert. *Folk Songs of the Blue Ridge Mounains.* New York: Oak Publications, 1968.

Shoemaker (1923)   Shoemaker, Henry W. *North Pennsylvania Minstrelsy.*
                        Altoona: Times Tribune, 1923.

Shoemaker (1931)   _____ . *Mountain Minstrelsy of Pennsylvania.* Philadelphia:
                        Newman F. McGirr, 1931.

Smith   Smith, Reed. *South Carolina Ballads, with a Study of the Tradi-
                        tional Ballad Today.* Cambridge: Harvard University
                        Press, 1928.

Smith & Rufty   _____ , and Hilton Rufty. *American Anthology of Old World
                        Ballads.* New York: J. Fischer & Brothers, 1937.

Spaeth   Spaeth, Sigmund. *Read 'em and Weep: The Songs You Forgot to
                        Remember.* Garden City, New York: Doubleday, Page,
                        1926.

Stout   Stout, Earl J. *Folklore from Iowa.* New York: American
                        Folklore Society, 1936.

Sturgis & Hughes   Sturgis, Edith B. and Robert Hughes. *Songs from the Hills of
                        Vermont.* New York: G. Schirmer, 1919.

Sulzer   Sulzer, Elmer G. *Twenty-Five Kentucky Folk Ballads.*
                        Lexington, Kentucky: Transylvania Press, 1936.

Talley   Talley, Thomas W. *Negro Folk Hymns.* 1922. Reprint, Port
                        Washington, New York: Kennikat Press, Inc., 1968.

Thomas (1931)   Thomas, Jean. *Devil's Ditties.* 1931. Reprint, Detroit: Gale
                        Research Company, 1976.

Thomas (1939)   _____ . *Ballad Makin' in the Mountains of Kentucky.* 1939.
                        Reprint, New York: Oak Publications, Inc., 1964.

Thomas & Leeder   _____ , and Joseph A. Leeder. *The Singin' Gatherin!* New
                        York: Silver Burdett Co., 1939.

Thompson   Thompson, Harold W. *Body, Boots and Britches: Folktales,
                        Ballads and Speech from Country New York.* 1940.
                        Reprint, Syracuse: Syracuse University Press, 1979.

Thompson & Cutting   _____ , and Edith E. Cutting. *A Pioneer Songster: Texts From
                        the Stevens-Douglass Manuscript of Western New York
                        1841–1856.* Ithaca, New York: Cornell University Press,
                        1958.

Thorp   Thorp, N. Howard "Jack". *Songs of the Cowboys.* 1921.
                        Reprint, Lincoln, Nebraska: University of Nebraska
                        Press, 1984.

Warner   Warner, Anne. *Traditional American Folk Songs from the Anne
                        & Frank Warner Collection.* Syracuse: Syracuse Univer-
                        sity Press, 1984.

Wells   Wells, Evelyn Kendrick. *The Ballad Tree.* New York: Ronald
                        Press, 1950.

Wheeler   Wheeler, Mary. *Kentucky Mountain Folk Songs.* Boston: The
                        Boston Music Company, 1937.

White   White, Newman Ivey. *American Negro Folk-Songs.* 1928.
                        Reprint, Hatboro, Pennsylvania: Folklore Associates,
                        1965.

Williams   Williams, Alfred. *Folk-Songs of the Upper Thames.* London:
                        Duckworth, 1923.

Wilson   Wilson, Charles Morrow. *Backwoods America.* Chapel Hill:
                        University of North Carolina Press, 1934.

Wyman & Brockway   Wyman, Loraine and Howard Brockway. *Lonesome Tunes:
                        Folk Songs from the Kentucky Mountains.* New York:
                        H. W. Gray Co., 1916.

Humorous Ballads

Billy Grimes

A. Belden, p. 251.
   Brown II, p. 466.
   Brown IV, p. 248.
   Chappell, p. 134.
   Cohen & Seeger, p. 74.
   Davis (1949), p. 234.
   Gardner & Chickering, p. 477.
   Hudson, p. 281.
   Pound, p. 205.
   Sharp, II, p. 248.
   Shoemaker (1923), p. 61.

C. Shelor Family   Victor 20865

D. I. G. Greer   *Anglo-American Songs and Ballads.* Library
                                         of Congress AAFS L14.
   The New Lost City Ramblers   *The New Lost City Ramblers. Volume Four.*
                                         Folkways FA 2399.
   —   *Old-Timey Music.* Disc D-102.

Four Nights Drunk

A. Abrahams-Foss, p. 108.
   Barry, p. 315.
   Belden, p. 89.
   Boette, p. 14.
   Brewster, p. 149.
   Bronson, p. 459.
   Brown II, p. 181.
   Brown IV, p. 103.
   Burton & Manning II, pp. 11, 65.
   Carey, p. 109.
   Chappell, p. 41.
   Chase, p. 118.
   Combs-Wilgus, p. 207.
   Cox, p. 154.
   Creighton & Senior, p. 91.
   Davis (1929), p. 485.
   Davis (1949), p. 31.

Davis (1960), p. 300.
Eddy, p. 82.
Emrich (1974), p. 338.
Finger, p. 161.
Flanders, IV, p. 63.
Gainer, p. 86.
Henry (1934), p. 14.
Henry (1938), p. 119.
Henry & Matteson, p. 14.
Hubbard, p. 34.
Hudson, p. 122.
Leisy, p. 111.
Linscott, p. 261.
MacKenzie (1928), p. 62.
Moore & Moore, p. 120.
Morris, p. 317.
Owens (1950), p. 65.
Parler, p. 17.
Parsons (1918), p. 162.
Randolph II, p. 225.
Randolph III, I, p. 181.
Roberts (1974), p. 97.
Rosenberg, p. 100.
Scarborough (1937), p. 231.
Seeger, p. 22.
Sharp, I, p. 267.
Smith, p. 159.
Stout, p. 13.

B. Cray, Ed. *The Erotic Muse.* New York: Oak Publications, 1969, p. 6.
  Palmer, Edgar A. *G.I. Songs: Written, Composed and/or Collected by Men in the Service.* New York: Sheridan House, Inc., 1944, p. 165.
  Shay, Frank. *More Pious Friends and Drunken Companions.* New York: The Macaulay Company, 1928.

C. John Evans   Brunswick 237
   Emmett Bankston and Red Henderson   Okeh 45292
   Earl Johnson and His Dixie Entertainers   Okeh 45090
   Coley Jones and Dallas String Band   Columbia 14889D
   Wade Mainer   Blue Ridge 109
   Mustard and Gravy   Bluebird 7905
   Earl Rogers   Musicraft MU 68
   Gid Tanner and Riley Puckett   Bluebird 5748

D. Coley Jones and Dallas String Band   *Anthology of American Folk Music. Volume One. Ballads.* Folkways FA 2951.

   Ewan MacColl and A. L. Lloyd   *The English and Scottish Popular Ballads.* Riverside RLP-21.

   Wade Mainer   *Songs of Love, Courtship, and Marriage.* Library of Congress. LBC 2.

Hattie Presnell	*The Traditional Music of Beech Mountain, North Carolina: Vol. 1.* Folk-Legacy FSA-22.
Orrin Rice	*Anglo-American Songs and Ballads.* Library of Congress AFS L12.
Pete Seeger	*American Favorite Ballads, Vol. 3.* Folkways FA 2322.

Frog Went A-Courtin'

A. Arnold, p. 12.
　Belden, p. 494.
　Cox, p. 471.
　Davis (1949), p. 208.
　Eddy, p. 137.
　Gardner & Chickering, p. 455.
　Henry (1934), p. 230.
　Henry (1938), p. 396.
　Hubbard, p. 387.
　Hudson, p. 282.
　Jones (1980), p. 92.
　Leisy, p. 234.
　Linscott, p. 199.
　MacKenzie (1928), p. 373.
　Randolph III, I, p. 402.
　Sandburg, p. 143.
　Scarborough (1937), p. 245.
　Seeger, p. 56.
　Sharp, II, p. 312.
　Sturgis & Hughes, p. 18.
　Talley, p. 190.
　Thomas (1931), p. 154.
　White, p. 176.
　Williams, p. 133.
　Wyman & Brockway, p. 25.

B. Cuccinello, Louis S. "The Frog Went a-Courting," *Southern Folklore Quarterly* (1962), 26: 97–106.
　Mitcham, Mildred B. "Another Version of 'The Frog's Courting,'" *Hoosier Folklore* (1946), 5: 85–92.
　Payne, Leonidas Warren, Jr. "The Frog's Courting," *Texas Folklore Society Publications* (1926), 5: 5–48.
　Raph, Theodore. *The Songs We Sang: A Treasury of American Popular Music.* Cranbury, New Jersey: A. S. Barnes and Co., Inc., 1964, p. 29.

| C. Anne, Judy and Zeke Canova | Brunswick 264 |
| Nelson Eddy | Victor 571 |

Harp Singers	Musicraft 41
Lewis James	Victor 22134
Bradley Kincaid	Supertone 9209
	Silvertone 5188
	Silvertone 8219
	Gennett 6462
	Champion 15466
	Conqueror 7889
John Jacob Niles	Victor VM-718
	Disc 733
Old Harp Singers	Musicraft 222
Chubby Parker	Conqueror 7889

D. Pleaz Mobley — *Anglo-American Songs and Ballads.* Library of Congress. AFS L12.

Chubby Parker — *Anthology of American Folk Music. Vol. 1— Ballads.* Folkways FA 2951.

Almeda Riddle — *Granny Riddle's Songs and Ballads.* Minstrel JD-203.

— *Songs and Ballads of the Ozarks.* Vanguard VRS 9158.

Jean Ritchie — *Field Trip.* Collector Limited Edition 1201.

Tex Ritter — *Deck of Cards.* Camay CA 3044.

Mike and Peggy Seeger — *American Folk Songs for Children.* Rounder 8001-8003.

Pete Seeger — *American Favorite Ballads, Vol. 4.* Folkways FA 2323.

Doc Watson — *Home Again.* Vanguard VSD 79239.

The Girl with the Waterfall

A. Davis (1949), p. 144.
   Henry (1938), p. 307.
   Randolph III, III, p. 110.

I Wish I Was Single Again

A. Arnold, p. 77.
   Belden, p. 437.
   Burton & Manning II, p. 13.
   Chappell, p. 133.
   Combs-Wilgus, p. 211.
   Eddy, p. 181.
   Gainer, p. 144.

Gardner & Chickering, p. 479.
Hubbard, p. 242.
Leisy, p. 177.
Owens (1983), p. 74.
Pound, p. 207.
Rosenberg, p. 117.
Sandburg, p. 47.
Shellans, p. 20.
Warner, p. 301.

B. *The Frank C. Brown Collection of North Carolina Folklore. Volume 3. Folk Songs.* Edited by
Henry M. Belden and Arthur Palmer Hudson. Durham: Duke University Press,
1952, p. 37.

Campbell, Marie. "Answering-Back Song Ballads," *Tennessee Folklore Society Bulletin*
(1958), 24: 3–10.

_____ . "Play-Party Tunes and Fritter-Minded Ballads," *Tennessee Folklore Society
Bulletin* (1939), 5: 17–48, p. 34.

Ford, Ira W. *Traditional Music of America.* 1940. Reprint, Hatboro, Pennsylvania:
Folklore Associates, 1965, p. 327.

C. Jim Burke (Pseudonym for Luther Ossenbrink)	Supertone 9492
Vernon Dalhart (Pseudonym for Marion Try Slaughter)	Cameo 1237
	Romeo 465
	Lincoln 2702
J. D. Foster & J. D. James	Supertone 9260
	Gennett 6434
Sid Harkreader	Vocalion 15035
Kelly Harrell	Victor 19563
	Victor 20242
Lulu Belle and Scotty	Vocalion 04772
Frank Luther	Decca DE 25
John Jacob Niles	Victor VM824
Riley Puckett	Columbia 15036-D
Welby Toomey	Gennett 3202

D. Vernon Dalhart (Pseudonym for Marion Try Slaughter)	*Vernon Dalhart 1921–1927.* Golden Olden Classics 701.
Kelly Harrell	*The Complete Kelly Harrell Volume 1.* Bear Family 15508.
Joan O'Bryant	*American Ballads and Folk Songs.* Folkways FA 2338.
Molly O'Day	*Radio Favorites.* Old Homestead OHCS 140.
Riley Puckett	*Waiting For the Evening Mail.* County 411.

Old Judge Duffy

B. Toelken, Barre J.   *The Dynamics of Folklore.* Boston: Houghton
                                           Mifflin Company, 1979, p. 351.

D. Van Holyoak   *Tioga Jim.* Rounder 0108.

The Rattlesnake Song

A. Belden, p. 299.
  Brewster, p. 322.
  Brown II, p. 489.
  Brown IV, p. 265.
  Eddy, p. 248.
  Gardner & Chickering, p. 120.
  Leach, p. 720.
  Leisy, p. 305.
  Linscott, p. 285.
  Lomax, A., p. 13.
  Pound, p. 97.
  Randolph III, III, p. 168.
  Scott, p. 156.
  Shoemaker (1923), p. 126.
  Warner, p. 91.
  White, p. 245.

B. Coffin, Tristram P. "On a Peak in Massachusetts: the Literary and Aesthetic
    Approach," in *A Good Tale and a Bonnie Tune,* ed. Mody C. Boatright *et al.,* pp. 201–
    209.
  Loomis, Marjorie C. "Songs: 'Springfield Mountain,' " *New York Folklore Quarterly*
    (1955), 11: 66–68.
  Moore, Arthur K. "A Springfield Mountain Composite," *Southern Folklore Quarterly*
    (1950), 14: 215–219.

C. American Ballad Singers   Victor V-P41
  Bascom Lamar Lunsford   Folkways Folk FP
                                           40
  The Old Harp Singers   Musicraft MU-
                                         222-B

D. Noble Cowden   *Not Far From Here: Traditional Tales and Songs
                              Recorded in the Arkansas Ozarks.*
                              Arkansas Traditions. No number.
  Sam Hinton   *The Wandering Folk Song.* Folkways FA 2401.

Bascom Lamar Lunsford   *Smoky Mountain Ballads.* Folkways FA 2040.
Frank Warner   *Come All You Good People.* Minstrel JD 204.

Three Jolly Welshmen

A. Belden, p. 246.
   Brown II, p. 460.
   Chappell, p. 174.
   Cohen & Seeger, p. 184.
   Cox, p. 478.
   Davis (1949), p. 198.
   Eddy, p. 208.
   Linscott, p. 290.
   Randolph III, I, p. 328.
   Scarborough (1925), p. 57.
   Williams, p. 179.

C. Byrd Moore & His Hot Shots   Columbia 15496

D. New Lost City Ramblers   *New Lost City Ramblers, Vol. 3.* Folkways FA 2398.

The Wife in Wether's Skin

A. Abrahams-Foss, p. 167.
   Arnold, p. 110.
   Barry, p. 322.
   Belden, p. 92.
   Boette, p. 18.
   Brewster, p. 151.
   Bronson, p. 466.
   Brown II, p. 185.
   Brown IV, p. 113.
   Burton & Manning I, p. 56.
   Bush I, p. 80.
   Cazden, p. 36.
   Chase, p. 122.
   Cox, p. 159.
   Creighton & Senior, p. 94.
   Davis (1929), p. 497.
   Davis (1949), p. 32.
   Davis (1960), p. 305.
   Downes & Siegmeister, p. 226.

Flanders, IV, p. 76.
Flanders-Olney, p. 221.
Gainer, p. 90.
Grover, p. 68.
Henry (1938), p. 125.
Hubbard, p. 38.
Hudson, p. 123.
Ives, p. 178.
Leach, p. 658.
Lomax, A., p. 167.
Moore & Moore, p. 125.
Morris, p. 322.
Owens (1950), p. 66.
Owens (1983), p. 71.
Parler, p. 10.
Pound, p. 16.
Randolph III, I, p. 187.
Ritchie (1965), p. 76.
Sharp, I, p. 271.
Smith & Rufty, p. 49.
Warner, pp. 136, 264.
Wells, p. 121.

C. Richard Dyer-Bennet	Remington 199-34
Burl Ives	Columbia C-103
Chubby Parker	Gennett 6077

D. Hedy West	*Old Times and Hard Times.* Folk-Legacy FSA-32.

Willy Weaver

A. Brewster, p. 360.
   Henry (1938), p. 304.
   MacKenzie (1928), p. 328.
   Sharp, II, p. 207.
   Shoemaker (1931), p. 135.
   Warner, p. 139.
   Williams, p. 106.

B. Patterson, Daniel W. "A Sheaf of North Carolina Folksongs," *North Carolina Folklore* (1956), 4: 23–31, 23.

D. Loman Cansler	*Folksongs of the Midwest.* Folkways FH 5330.

Songs and Ballads of the Ozarks. Vanguard
                                         V RS 9158.

Murder Ballads

Little Marian Parker

A. Brown II, p. 603.
   Burt, p. 65.

C. Blind Andy (Pseudonym for Andrew Jenkins)   Okeh 45197
   Vernon Dalhart   Perfect 12429
                                                       Paramount 3091

D. Vernon Dalhart   *Old Time Songs 1925–1930.*
                                                          Davis Unlimited DU
                                                          33030.
   —   *Vernon Dalhart, Vol. III.* Old
                                                          Homestead OCHS-
                                                          167.

Little Mary Fagan

A. Arnold, p. 74.
   Brown II, p. 598.
   Brown IV, p. 295.
   Burt, p. 61.
   Cambiaire, p. 104.
   Eddy, p. 252.
   Gardner & Chickering, p. 352.
   Morris, p. 81.

B. Carter, Isabel Gordon. "Some Songs and Ballads from Tennessee and North Carolina,"
      Journal of American Folklore (1933), 46: 22–50, 39.
   Dinnerstein, Leonard. *The Leo Frank Case.* New York: Columbia University Press, 1968,
      p. 166.
   Schmitz, R. M. "Leo Frank and Mary Phagan," *Journal of American Folklore* (1947), 60:
      59–61.
   Snyder, F. B. "Leo Frank and Mary Phagan," *Journal of American Folklore* (1917), 30:
      264–266.

C. Rosa Lee Carson   Okeh 40446
    Vernon Dalhart   Okeh 40568
                                               Columbia 15031-
                                               D

D. Vernon Dalhart   *Ballads and Railroad Songs.*
                                           Old Homestead OHCS-129.

Lord Barnie

A. Abrahams-Foss, p. 97.
    Arnold, p. 60.
    Barry, p. 122.
    Belden, p. 34.
    Brewster, p. 166.
    Bronson, p. 174.
    Brown II, p. 67.
    Brown IV, p. 29.
    Bush I, p. 75.
    Cambiaire, p. 28.
    Chappell, p. 21.
    Cox, p. 42.
    Creighton & Senior, p. 36.
    Davis (1929), p. 182.
    Davis (1949), p. 13.
    Davis (1960), p. 111.
    Gainer, p. 37.
    Henry (1938), p. 145.
    Hudson, p. 77.
    Jekyll, p. 96.
    Leach, p. 229.
    Moore & Moore, p. 47.
    Morris, p. 263.
    Owens (1950), p. 44.
    Randolph II, p. 203.
    Randolph III, I, p. 90.
    Randolph & Cohen, p. 28.
    Sandburg, p. 64.
    Scarborough (1937), p. 134.
    Sharp, I, p. 101.
    Smith, p. 107.
    Smith & Rufty, p. 15.
    Wells, p. 152.

B. Wimberly, Lowry Charles. "Two Traditional Ballads," *American Speech* (1927), 3: 114–
    118.

C. Jimmie Tarlton Columbia 15763-
D

D. Darby & Tarlton *Darby & Tarlton.* Old Timey OT 112.
Jimmie Tarlton *Steel Guitar Rag.* Testament T-3302.

Lula Viers

A. Roberts (1978), p. 140.
Thomas (1939), p. 144.

D. Bruce Buckley *Ohio Valley Ballads.* Folkways FA 2025.

Nellie Cropsey

A. Brown II, p. 717.
Brown IV, p. 327.
Chappell, p. 108.

B. Quillin, Brenda Joyce. "Nell Cropsy Died—But How?" *North Carolina Folklore Journal*
(1974), 22: 43–54.

D. Beck Etheridge *Between the Sound and the Sea.* Folkways FS
3848.

Pearl Bryan

A. Brewster, p. 286.
Brown II, p. 588.
Brown IV, p. 292.
Burt, p. 31.
Burton & Manning I, p. 77.
Cambiaire, p. 109.
Combs-Wilgus, p. 174.
Cox, p. 200.
Eddy, p. 241.
Finger, p. 80.
Henry (1938), p. 209.

Jones (1980), p. 105.
Leach, p. 788.
Morris, p. 79.
Neely, p. 158.
Randolph III, II, p. 48.

B. Cohen, Anne B. *Poor Pearl, Poor Girl!: The Murdered-Girl Stereotype in Ballad and Newspaper.* Austin: The University of Texas Press, 1973.
Vlach, John M. " 'Pearl Bryan': Two Ballads in One Tradition," *Journal of Country Music* (1972), 3: 45–61.
Wilson, Ann Scott. "Pearl Bryan," *Southern Folklore Quarterly* (1939), 3: 15–19.

C. Burnett and Rutherford   Columbia 15113-D

Roy Harvey and Bob Hoke   Gennett 887
       Supertone 9246
       Silvertone 5181
       Silvertone 8147
Bradley Kincaid   Supertone 9404
       Gennett 6823
       Champion 15731

D. Burnett and Rutherford   *Old Time Ballads From the Southern Mountains.* County 522.
Bradley Kincaid   *Mountain Ballads and Old Time Songs. Album Number 4.* Bluebonnett BL112.
Gladys Pace   *I Kind of Believe It's a Gift: Field Recordings of Traditional Music From Southcentral Kentucky.* Meriweather 1001-2.
Obray Ramsey   *Sings Folksongs From the Gateways to the Great Smokies.* Prestige International 13030.

La Hija Desobediente

B. Hansen, Terence L. "*Corridos* in Southern California," *Western Folklore* (1959), 18: 203–232, p. 224.
Robb, John Donald. *Hispanic Folk Music of New Mexico and the Southwest: A Self-Portrait of a People.* Norman: University of Oklahoma Press, 1980, p. 125.

A. Abrahams-Riddle, p. 139.
   Barry, p. 134.
   Belden, p. 48.
   Brewster, p. 71.
   Bronson, p. 189.
   Brown II, p. 79.
   Brown IV, p. 40.
   Chappell, p. 25.
   Cox, p. 65.
   Cutting, p. 64.
   Davis (1929), p. 221.
   Davis (1949), p. 15.
   Davis (1960), p. 138.
   Eddy, p. 34.
   Emrich (1974), p. 285.
   Flanders, II, p. 122.
   Flanders-Olney, p. 80.
   Gainer, p. 42.
   Gardner & Chickering, p. 40.
   Hudson, p. 87.
   Jones (1984), p. 194.
   Leach, p. 247.
   MacKenzie (1919), p. 124.
   MacKenzie (1928), p. 25.
   McGill, p. 71.
   Moore & Moore, p. 54.
   Neely, p. 141.
   Parler, p. 39.
   Pound, p. 40.
   Randolph I, p. 181.
   Randolph III, I, p. 108.
   Ritchie (1965), p. 18.
   Rosenberg, p. 33.
   Scarborough (1937), p. 103.
   Sharp, I, p. 139.
   Wells, p. 106.
   Wyman & Brockway, p. 94.

B. "Fair Margaret and False William," *Journal of American Folklore* (1906), 19: 281–282.

C. Professor and Mrs. I. G. Greer   Paramount 3236

D. Professor and Mrs. I. G. Greer   *Gambler's Lament: Old-Time Songs and
                                            Ballads from the Southern States.*
                                            Country Turtle CT-6001.
   Max Hunter   *Max Hunter of Springfield, Missouri.* Folk-
                                            Legacy FSA-11.

198

The Seventh Sister

A. Arnold, p. 54.
   Barry, p. 14.
   Belden, p. 5.
   Brewster, p. 31.
   Bronson, p. 15.
   Brown II, p. 15.
   Brown IV, p. 4.
   Bush II, p. 90.
   Chappell, p. 12.
   Cox, p. 3.
   Creighton & Senior, p. 2.
   Cutting, p. 61.
   Davis (1929), p. 62.
   Davis (1949), p. 4.
   Davis (1960), p. 16.
   Eddy, p. 6.
   Fauset, p. 109.
   Flanders, I, p. 82.
   Flanders-Olney, pp. 4, 129.
   Fowke, p. 102.
   Gainer, p. 6.
   Gardner & Chickering, p. 31.
   Greenleaf & Mansfield, p. 3.
   Grover, p. 25.
   Henry (1938), p. 32.
   High, p. 10.
   Hubbard, p. 1.
   Hudson, p. 61.
   Leach, p. 53.
   Lomax, A., p. 18.
   MacKenzie (1919), p. 93.
   MacKenzie (1928), p. 3.
   Manny & Wilson, p. 202.
   Moore & Moore, p. 12.
   Morris, p. 237.
   Owens (1950), p. 35.
   Parsons (1923), p. 128.
   Peacock, I, p. 206.
   Peters, p. 199.
   Randolph II, p. 216.
   Randolph III, I, p. 41.
   Randolph & Cohen, p. 16.
   Ritchie (1965), p. 8.
   Roberts (1978), p. 8.

Rosenberg, p. 67.
Sandburg, p. 60.
Scarborough (1925), p. 43.
Scarborough (1937), p. 126.
Sharp, I, p. 6.
Smith, p. 97.
Warner, p. 130.
Wyman & Brockway, p. 82.

B. Barbour, Frances M. "Some Fusions in Missouri Ballads," *Journal of American Folklore* (1936), 49: 207–214, 213.
   Kemppinen, Iivar. *The Ballad of Lady Isabel and the False Knight.* Helsinki: Suomen Kulttuurirahasto, 1954.
   Nygard, Holger Olof. *The Ballad of Heer Halewijn; Its Forms and Variations in Western Europe; a Study of the History and Nature of a Ballad Tradition.* Helsinki: Suomalainen Tiedeakatemia, 1958.
   _____ . "Ballad Source Study: Child Ballad No. 4 an Exemplar," *Journal of American Folklore* (1955), 68: 141–152.

C. Richard Dyer-Bennet   Decca A-573

D. Jumbo Brightwell   *English Folk Songs.* Columbia KL 206.
   LaRena Clark   *Traditional Songs of Ontario.* Topic 12T140.
   Fred Jordan   *Child Ballads. I.* Caedmon TC 1145.
   Jean Ritchie   *British Traditional Ballads (Child Ballads) in the Southern Mountains. II.* Folkways FA2302.
   _____ .   *Kentucky Mountain Songs.* Elektra EKL 125.
   Clara Hawks Tracy   *Wolf River Songs.* Folkways FM 4001.

Sonny Hugh

A. Arnold, p. 42.
   Belden, p. 69.
   Brewster, p. 128.
   Bronson, p. 294.
   Brown II, p. 155.
   Brown IV, p. 82.
   Burton & Manning I, p. 1.
   Cox, p. 120.
   Davis (1929), p. 400.
   Davis (1949), p. 25.
   Davis (1960), p. 229.
   Eddy, p. 66.
   Flanders, III, p. 119.
   Flanders-Olney, p. 30.

Gainer, p. 68.
Henry (1938), p. 102.
Henry & Matteson, p. 22.
Hubbard, p. 24.
Hudson, p. 116.
Killion & Waller, p. 258.
Leach, p. 425.
Lomax, A., p. 511.
MacColl & Seeger, p. 86.
Moore & Moore, p. 89.
Morris, p. 302.
Parler, p. 35.
Peters, p. 198.
Pound, p. 13.
Rainey, p. 8.
Randolph III, I, p. 148.
Randolph & Cohen, p. 47.
Roberts (1978), p. 67.
Scarborough (1925), p. 53.
Scarborough (1937), p. 171.
Sharp, I, p. 122.
Smith, p. 148.

B. Burton, Thomas G. " 'Sir Hugh' in Sullivan County," *Tennessee Folklore Society Bulletin* (1965), 31: 42–47.

Hippensteel, Faith. " 'Sir Hugh': the Hoosier Contribution to the Ballad," *Indiana Folklore* (1969), 2: 75–140.

Ridley, Florence II. "A Tale Told Too Often," *Western Folklore* (1967), 26: 153–156.

Stamper, Frances C., and William Hugh Jansen. " 'Water Birch': An American Variant of 'Hugh of Lincoln'," *Journal of American Folklore* (1958), 71: 16–22.

Woodall, James R. " 'Sir Hugh': a Study in Balladry," *Southern Folklore Quarterly* (1955), 19: 77–84.

C. Nelstone's Hawaiians   Victor V-40193

D. Ollie Gilbert   *Aunt Ollie Gilbert Sings Old Folksongs to Her Friends.* Rackensack RLP 495.

Nelstone's Hawaiians   *Anthology of American Folk Music. Volume One. Ballads.* Folkways FA 2951.

The Two Sisters

A. Abrahams-Foss, p. 20.
Barry, p. 40.
Belden, p. 16.
Boette, p. 32.

Brewster, p. 42.
Bronson, p. 34.
Brown II, p. 32.
Brown IV, p. 13.
Burton & Manning I, p. 29.
Carey, p. 94.
Chappell, p. 13.
Cox, p. 20.
Davis (1929), p. 93.
Davis (1949), p. 6.
Davis (1960), p. 35.
Eddy, p. 17.
Emrich (1974), p. 255.
Flanders, I, p. 150.
Flanders-Olney, p. 209.
Gainer, p. 10.
Gardner & Chickering, p. 32.
Greenleaf & Mansfield, p. 9.
Henry (1938), p. 39.
Hubbard, p. 5.
Hudson, p. 68.
Jameson, p. 41.
Jones (1980), p. 88.
Jones (1984), p. 201.
Leach, p. 74.
Leisy, p. 330.
Lomax, p. 184.
MacColl & Seeger, p. 51.
Moore & Moore, p. 19.
Morris, p. 243.
Niles I, p. 36.
Pound, p. 11.
Raine, p. 118.
Randolph II, p. 211.
Randolph III, I, p. 50.
Randolph & Cohen, p. 18.
Ritchie (1965), p. 63.
Roberts (1978), p. 16.
Scarborough (1937), p. 164.
Sharp, I, p. 26.
Smith & Rufty, p. 2.
Stout, p. 1.
Thomas (1931), p. 70.
Thomas & Leeder, p. 76.
Thompson, p. 393.
Warner, p. 243.

B. Brewster, Paul G. *The Two Sisters*. Helsinki: Suomalainen Tiedeakatemia, 1953.
   Foss, George. "More on a Unique and Anomalous Version of 'The Two Sisters'," *Southern Folklore Quarterly* (1964), 28: 119–133.

C. Richard Dyer-Bennet	Remington 199-34
Richard Hayward	Decca G-20234
Bradley Kincaid	Supertone 9212
	Silvertone 8221
Andrew Rowan Summers	Columbia 408

D. Horton Barker	*Anglo-American Ballads.* Library of Congress L 7.
Loman Cansler	*Missouri Folksongs.* Folkways H 5324.
Lula Curry	*American Folk Song Festival.* Folkways FA 2358.
Richard Dyer-Bennet	*Dyer-Bennet.* DYB 6000.
Bascom Lamar Lunsford	*Minstrel of the Appalachians.* Riverside RLP 12-645.
Lee Monroe Presnell	*The Traditional Music of Beech Mountain, Vol. 1.* Folk-Legacy FSA-22.
Jean Ritchie	*British Traditional Ballads (Child Ballads) in the Southern Mountains. II.* Folkways FA 2302.
_____.	*Child Ballads Traditional in the United States (I).* Library of Congress L 57.
Kilby Snow	*Country Songs and Tunes With Autoharp.* Folkways FA 3902.
Ellen Stekert	*Songs of a New York Lumberjack.* Folkways FA 2354.
Dan Tate	*Virginia Traditions: Ballads From British Tradition.* BRI-002.
The Williams Family	*All In the Family.* Arkansas Traditions 004.

Ole Banghum

A. Abrahams-Foss, p. 60.
    Belden, p. 29.
    Bronson, p. 70.
    Chase, p. 126.
    Davis (1929), p. 125.
    Davis (1949), p. 9.
    Davis (1960), p. 72.
    Flanders, I, p. 226.
    Flanders-Olney, p. 60.
    Gainer, p. 24.
    Leach, p. 100.
    Lomax, A., p. 510.
    McGill, p. 79.
    Moore & Moore, p. 29.
    Parler, p. 45.
    Randolph III, I, p. 72.

Ritchie (1965), p. 91.
Rosenberg, p. 117.
Scarborough (1925), p. 51.
Scarborough (1937), p. 191.
Sharp, I, p. 55.
Smith & Rufty, p. 4.

C. Bentley Ball	Columbia 90055
Richard Dyer-Bennet	Vocalion VOX-632
	Keynote K-108
Andrew Rowan Summers	Columbia 408

D. Samuel Harmon and G. D. Vowell	*Child Ballads Traditional in the United States (1).* Library of Congress L 57.
Buna Hicks	*The Traditional Music of Beech Mountain, Vol. 1.* Folk-Legacy FSA-22.
The Kimble Family	*Blue Ridge Barn Dance.* County 746.
Jean Ritchie	*British Traditional Ballads in the Southern Mountains, Vol. 1.* Folkways FA 2301.
Peggy Seeger	*Popular Ballads.* Folk-Lyric FL120.

Ballads of Tragedies and Disasters

The Romish Lady

A. Arnold, p. 19.
  Belden, p. 450.
  Brewster, p. 257.
  Brown II, p. 213.
  Brown IV, p. 132.
  Eddy, p. 220.
  Gardner & Chickering, p. 363.
  Hudson, p. 137.
  Morris, p. 388.
  Owens (1950), p. 284.
  Pound, p. 63.
  Randolph III, IV, p. 32.
  Scarborough (1937), p. 176.

B. Jackson, George Pullen. *Spiritual Folk-Songs of Early America.* 1937. Reprint. New York: Dover Publications, Inc., 1964, p. 27.

Schaladi

A. Belden, p. 308.
Brewster, p. 181.
Brown II, p. 492.
Brown IV, p. 267.
Burton & Manning, p. 52.
Gardner & Chickering, p. 126.
High, p. 32.
Hubbard, p. 74.
Leach, p. 723.
Leisy, p. 375.
Lomax, A., p. 94.
Morris, p. 114.
Owens (1950), p. 98.
Rainey, p. 46.
Randolph III, IV, p. 105.
Randolph & Cohen, p. 528.
Stout, p. 51.
Thompson, p. 374.

D. I. G. Greer — *Anglo-American Songs and Ballads.* Library of Congress L 14.

Almeda Riddle — *Songs and Ballads of the Ozarks.* Vanguard VRS 9158.

Vern Smelser — *Fine Times At Our House.* Folkways FS 3809.

Betty Smith — *Songs Traditionally Sung in North Carolina.* Folk-Legacy FSA-53.

Three Perished in the Snow

A. Arnold, p. 98.
Cazden, p. 50.

The Titanic

A. Brown II, p. 662.
Brown IV, p. 314.

Gardner & Chickering, p. 295.
Henry (1938), p. 427.
Leisy, p. 322.
Randolph III, IV, p. 144.
Sandburg, p. 254.
White, p. 347.

C. Richard "Rabbit" Brown   Victor 35840-B
   A. P. Carter Family   Acme-1000
   Vernon Dalhart   Challenge 155
   William & Versey Smith   Paramount 12505
   Ernest V. Stoneman   Okeh 40288

D. Roy Acuff   *American Folk Songs.* Hickory LPM 115.
   —   *The Best of Roy Acuff (Songs of the Smoky Mountains).* Capitol DS 1870.
   —   *Country Music Hall of Fame.* Hickory LPM 119.
   —   *Why Is Roy Acuff?* Hickory LPS 162.
   Rolf Cahn   *California Concert.* Folkways FA 2416.
   Vernon Dalhart   *Ballads and Railroad Songs.* Old Homestead OHCS-129.
   Darby & Tarlton   *New Birmingham Jail.* Folk Variety FV 12504.
   Leadbelly   *Leadbelly.* Folkways FA 2914.
   The Phipps Family   *The Phipps Family.* Folkways FA2375.
   Pete Seeger   *American Ballads.* Folkways FA 2319.
   Hobart Smith   *Hobart Smith of Saltville, Virginia.* Folk-Legacy FSA-17.
   William and Versey Smith   *Anthology of American Folk Music. Volume One. Ballads.* Folkways FH 2951.

The Vulture

D. Dee and Delta Hicks   *Ballads and Banjo Music From the Tennessee Cumberland Plateau.* County 789.

Ballads of the Supernatural

The Devil's Nine Questions

A. Abrahams-Foss, p. 86.
   Barry, p. 429.
   Boette, p. 36.
   Botkin (1949), p. 717.
   Bronson, p. 3.
   Brown IV, p. 331.
   Davis (1929), p. 59.
   Davis (1949), p. 3.
   Davis (1960), p. 1.
   Emrich (1974), p. 248.
   Flanders, I, p. 45.
   Gainer, p. 3.
   Ives, p. 38.
   Jekyll, p. 26.
   Leach, p. 47.
   Lomax, A., p. 180.
   Moore & Moore, p. 6.
   Wells, p. 169.

C. Burl Ives   Decca DEA-431.

D. Robert and Mary Gillihan   *Robert and Mary Gillihan.*
                                        No label name. 010069.
   Texas Gladden   *Anglo-American Ballads, Volume 1.*
                                        Library of Congress L1.
   —   *Virginia Traditions: Ballads from British Tradi-*
                                        tion. BRI-002.
   Frank Profitt   *Frank Profitt.* Folkways FA 2360.

The False Knight upon the Road

A. Barry, p. 11.
   Belden, p. 8.
   Brewster, p. 29.
   Bronson, p. 13.
   Creighton and Senior, p. 1.
   Davis (1929), p. 61.
   Davis (1949), p. 4.
   Davis (1960), p. 14.

Emrich (1974), p. 250.
Flanders-Olney, p. 46.
Manny & Wilson, p. 199.
Moore & Moore, p. 11.
Parler, p. 44.
Pound, p. 48.
Roberts (1974), p. 89.
Rosenberg, p. 34.
Sharp, I, p. 3.

B. Barry, Phillips. "British Ballads (Old World Ballads) in New England," Folk Song
    Society of the North-east (1936), 11: 8.

D. Mrs. Maud Long   *Anglo-American Songs and Ballads.* Library
                                         of Congress. AFS L21.

The House Carpenter

A. Abrahams-Foss, p. 25.
Abrahams-Riddle, p. 8.
Barry, p. 304.
Belden, p. 79.
Boette, p. 9.
Brewster, p. 136.
Bronson, p. 429.
Brown II, p. 171.
Brown IV, p. 95.
Burton & Manning I, p. 4, 65.
Burton & Manning II, pp. 3, 76, 105.
Bush I, p. 77.
Carey, p. 103.
Cazden, p. 82.
Chappell, p. 38.
Combs-Wilgus, p. 207.
Cox, p. 139.
Creighton (1971), p. 14.
Cutting, p. 69
Davis (1929), p. 439.
Davis (1949), p. 28.
Davis (1960), p. 270.
Dean, p. 55.
Eddy, p. 70.
Emrich (1974), p. 331.
Flanders, III, p. 287.
Flanders-Olney, p. 132.
Gainer, p. 80.
Gardner & Chickering, p. 54.

Henry (1934), p. 59.
Henry (1938), p. 116.
High, p. 16.
Hubbard, p. 28.
Hudson, p. 119.
Jones (1980), p. 87.
Leisy, p. 166.
Lomax, A., p. 182.
Moore & Moore, p. 112.
Morris, p. 311.
Owens (1950), p. 56.
Owens (1983), p. 33.
Peacock, III, p. 740.
Pound, p. 43.
Raim & Dunson, p. 24.
Rainey, p. 24.
Randolph II, p. 201.
Randolph III, I, p. 166.
Ritchie (1965), p. 90.
Rosenberg, p. 58.
Sandburg, p. 66.
Scarborough (1937), p. 150.
Sharp, I, p. 244.
Shellans, p. 30.
Smith & Rufty, p. 44.
Stout, p. 11.
Thomas (1931), p. 172.
Warner, p. 137.
Wilson, p. 96.
Wyman & Brockway, p. 54.

B. Burrison, John. " 'James Harris' in Britain Since Child," *Journal of American Folklore* (1967), 80: 271–284.

Burton, Thomas G. *Tom Ashley, Sam McGee, Bukka White: Tennessee Traditional Singers.* Knoxville: The University of Tennessee Press, 1981, p. 51.

Coffin, Tristram Potter, and Hennig Cohen. *Folklore: From the Working Folk of America.* Garden City, New York: Anchor Press, 1973, p. 77.

Gardner-Merwin, Alisoun. "The Ancestry of 'The House Carpenter,' " *Journal of American Folklore* (1971), 84: 414–427.

Hand, Wayland D. "Two Child Ballads in the West," *Western Folklore* (1959), 18: 42–45.

Lloyd, A. L., and Isabel Aretz de Ramon y Rivera. *Folk Songs of the Americas.* New York: Oak Publications, 1965, p. 50.

C. Clarence Ashley   Columbia 15654
Richard Dyer-Bennet   Keynote KE-518.
Texas Gladden and Hobart Smith   Disc 737
Bradley Kincaid   Bluebird 5255
                                                                      Superior 3338

D. Lena and Etta Armstrong	*The Traditional Music of Beech Mountain, North Carolina, Vol. 1.* Folk-Legacy FSA-22.
Clarence Ashley	*Anthology of American Folk Music. Volume One. Ballads.* Folkways FA 2951.
Clarence Ashley	*Old Time Music at Newport.* Vanguard 9147.
Clarence Ashley and Tex Isley	*Clarence Ashley and Tex Isley.* Folkways FA 2350.
Pearl Jacobs Borusky and Clay Walters	*Child Ballads Traditional in the United States II.* Library of Congress AFS L 58.
LaRena Clark	*Traditional Songs of Ontario.* Topic 12T140.
Noble Cowden	*Not Far From Here: Traditional Tales and Songs Recorded in the Arkansas Ozarks.* Arkansas Traditions (no number).
Texas Gladden	*Anglo-American Ballads.* Library of Congress AFS L 1.
Bradley Kincaid	*Favorite Ballads and Old Time Songs.* Old Homestead OHCS 155.
—	*Mountain Ballads and Old Time Songs. Number Three.* Bluebonnet BL 109.
Audrey McGuire	*Tennessee: The Folk Heritage Vol. 2 The Mountains.* TFS-103.
Joan O'Bryant	*American Ballads and Folk Songs.* Folkways FA 2338.
Almeda Riddle	*Songs and Ballads of the Ozarks.* Vanguard VRS 9158.
Jean Ritchie	*British Traditional Ballads in the Southern Mountains, Vol. 1.* Folkways FA 2301.
Dorothy Rorick	*Virginia Traditions: Ballads From British Tradition.* BRI-002.
Peggy Seeger	*Folk Songs of Courting and Complaint.* Folkways FP 49.
Pete Steele	*Banjo Tunes.* Folkways FS 3828.
Andrew Rowan Summers	*The Unquiet Grave and Other American Tragic Ballads.* Folkways FA 2364.
The Watson Family	*The Watson Family.* Folkways FA 2366.

J'ai Marié un Ouvrier

D. Beausoleil   *Allons à Lafayette* Arhoolie 5036

Lazarus

A. Belden, p. 447.
 Burton & Manning I, p. 42.

Cox, p. 407.
High, p. 31.
Randolph III, IV, p. 48.

B. Jackson, George Pullen. *White Spirituals in the Southern Uplands.* Chapel Hill, North
Carolina: University of North Carolina Press, 1933, p. 195.
_____ . *Spiritual Folk-Songs of Early America.* New York: Dover Publications, Inc.;
reissue of a work originally published in 1937, p. 36.

Mary Hebrew

A. Abrahams-Riddle, p. 114.
Arnold, p. 56.
Belden, p. 55.
Bronson, p. 206.
Brown II, p. 95.
Brown IV, p. 48.
Cambiaire, p. 121.
Chase, p. 116.
Cox, p. 88.
Davis (1929), p. 279.
Davis (1949), p. 17.
Davis (1960), p. 161.
Eddy, p. 46.
Emrich (1974), p. 291.
Flanders, II, p. 187.
Flanders-Olney, p. 64.
Fowke & Johnston, p. 24.
Fuson, p. 59.
Gainer, p. 51.
Henry (1938), p. 71.
High, p. 48.
Hudson, p. 93.
Leach, p. 263.
Lomax, A., p. 185.
McGill, p. 5.
Moore & Moore, p. 61.
Morris, p. 279.
Niles I, p. 14.
Owens (1950), p. 33.
Owens (1983), p. 29.
Palmer, p. 44.
Parler, p. 38.
Pound, p. 18.
Rainey, p. 9.
Randolph I, p. 180.
Randolph III, I, p. 122.
Ritchie (1965), p. 75.

Roberts (1978), p. 47.
Rosenberg, p. 137.
Scarborough (1937), p. 167.
Sharp, I, p. 150.
Smith & Rufty, p. 23.
Wells, p. 155.
Wheeler, p. 14.

C. Buell Kazee   Brunswick BR-
                                                  212.
   John Jacob Niles   Victor VM824.

D. Texas Gladden   *Child Ballads Traditional in the United States.*
                                     II. Library of Congress. L 58.
   I. G. Greer   *Anglo-American Ballads.* Library of
                                     Congress. L 7.
   Buell Kazee   *Kentucky Country.* Rounder 1037.
   Spence Moore   *Virginia Traditions: Ballads From British Tradi-*
                                     tion. BRI-002.
   Almeda Riddle   *Songs and Ballads of the Ozarks.* Vanguard
                                     VRS 9158.
   Jean Ritchie   *British Traditional Ballads in the Southern*
                                     Mountains, Vol. II. Folkways FA 2302.
   Hedy West   *Old Times and Hard Times.* Folk-Legacy FSA-
                                     32.

Two Brothers

A. Barry, p. 99.
   Belden, p. 33.
   Brewster, p. 55.
   Bronson, p. 129.
   Brown II, p. 49.
   Chappell, p. 17.
   Cox, p. 33.
   Creighton & Senior, p. 25.
   Davis (1929), p. 146.
   Davis (1949), p. 11.
   Davis (1960), p. 92.
   Eddy, p. 26.
   Emrich (1974), p. 270.
   Flanders, I, p. 316.
   Flanders-Olney, p. 96.
   Gainer, p. 30.
   High, p. 47.
   Hudson, p. 73.
   Leach, p. 164.

Linscott, p. 278.
McGill, p. 55.
Moore & Moore, p. 38.
Morris, p. 254.
Parler, p. 53.
Peacock, III, p. 827.
Pound, p. 45.
Randolph III, I, p. 76.
Rosenberg, p. 128.
Scarborough (1937), p. 166.
Sharp, I, p. 69.

B. Barry, Phillips. "The Two Brothers," *Bulletin of the Folk Song Society of the North-East* (1933), 5, 6.

C. Shep Ginandes   Elektra JH 508

D. Gladden, Texas   *Anglo-American Ballads.* Library of Congress L 7.

Sentimental Songs of Death and Dying

Daisy Deane

B. Cothran, Kay L. "Songs, Games and Memories of Mr. George W. Mitchell," *Tennessee Folklore Society Bulletin* (September, 1968), 34: 3, 70–71.
  Wolf, Edwin, II. *American Song Sheets, Slip Ballads, and Poetical Broadsides, 1850–1870: A Catalogue of the Collection of the Library Company of Philadelphia.* Philadelphia: Library Company of Philadelphia, 1963, p. 28.

C. Louis M. "Grandpa" Jones   King 834

D. Louis M. "Grandpa" Jones   *Grandpa Jones.* King 809.
   —   *24 Country Songs That Will Live Forever.* King 967.
   —   *The Legend.* Starday SR 200.

A. Brewster, p. 351.
   Cox, p. 395.
   Gardner & Chickering, p. 480.
   Henry (1938), p. 414.
   Hubbard, p. 128.
   Morris, p. 139.
   Neely, p. 223.
   Owens (1950), p. 145.
   Owens (1983), p. 63.
   Pound, p. 202.
   Shoemaker (1923), p. 135.
   Stout, p. 80.

B. Dugaw, Diane. " 'Dreams of the Past': A Collection of Ozark Songs and Tunes," *Mid-America Folklore* (1983), 11: 1–79, 29.
   Wellman, Manley Wade. *The Rebel Songster* (Charlotte, North Carolina: Heritage House, 1959), pp. 48–50.

C. Vernon Dalhart   Victor 20058
   Doc Hopkins   Decca 5983
   Bradley Kincaid   Supertone 9208
                                              Gennett 6363
                                              Champion 15502
                                              Silvertone 5187
                                              Silvertone 8218
   Obed Pickard   Columbia 15141-D

   Pickard Family   Conqueror 7517
   Ernest V. Stoneman   Okeh 45048
                                              Edison 51994
   Claude Sharpe and The Old Hickory   Columbia 20516
      Singers
   The Westerners   Musical Library 1321

D. Girls of the Golden West   *Songs of the West.* Old Homestead OHCS-143.

   Bradley Kincaid   *Old-Time Songs and Hymns, Vol. 4.* Old Homestead OHCS-317.

214

A. Davis (1949), p. 120.
   Kennedy, p. 131.
   Randolph III, IV, p. 162.
   Randolph & Cohen, p. 475.
   Stout, p. 74.

C. Fiddlin' John Carson   Okeh 7008
   Pete Cassell   Majestic 6007
   Vernon Dalhart   Columbia 15049-D
        Victor 19837
   Bradley Kincaid   Bluebird B-5895
   Marc Williams   Decca 5327
   George Reneau   Vocalion 14998
        Vocalion 5058

D. Vernon Dalhart   *Old Time Songs.* Davis Unlimited DU 33030.
   —   *Vernon Dalhart, Vol. III.* Old Homestead OCHS-167.
   Bill Harrell   *Ballads and Bluegrass.* Adelphi AD2013.
   Lena Hughes   *Queen of the Guitar Pickers and Her Flat Top Guitar.* Power PLP185.
   Bradley Kincaid   *Album Number Two.* Bluebonnet BL 105.
   Mac Wiseman   *The Golden Hits of Mac Wiseman.* Dot DLP25896.
   —   *New Traditions Vol. 2.* Vetco LP 509.
   —   *Songs of the Dear Old Days.* Hamilton HLP 167.

Little Bessie

A. Abrahams-Foss, p. 122.
   Burton & Manning II, p. 109.

C. Leroy Anderson   Champion 45059
   Blue Sky Boys   Bluebird 8017
   Tom Darby & Jimmie Tarlton   Columbia 15492
   Dixon Brothers   Montgomery Ward MW 7171
   Buell Kazee   Brunswick 215
        Vocalion 5231
   Holland Puckett (Pseudonym for Hartsell Watson)   Supertone 9324
   Kid Smith and Family   Victor 23576

D. Blue Sky Boys
—

Noble Cowden

Darby & Tarlton
Stanley Brothers
—

Blue Sky Boys. RCA AXM2-5525.
20 Country Classics. RCA Camden ADL2-
  0726.
Songs My Family Loves. Arkansas Tradi-
  tions 002.
Darby & Tarlton. Folk Variety FV 12504.
Old Country Church. Gusto GT-0084.
Old Time Camp Meeting. King K-750.

The Old Elm Tree

A. Belden, p. 221.
   Dean, p. 27.
   Randolph III, IV, p. 170.

B. Barry, Phillips. "The Transmission of Folk-Song," *Journal of American Folklore* (1914),
   27: 67–76, 69.

D. Floyd Holland

Stone County Singing. Shoestring Tape SGB
  1.

Orphan Girl

A. Belden, p. 277.
   Brewster, p. 291.
   Brown II, p. 388.
   Brown IV, p. 216.
   Chappell, p. 196.
   Cox, p. 446.
   Davis (1949), p. 117.
   Gainer, p. 118.
   Henry (1938), p. 373.
   Hubbard, p. 188.
   Kennedy, p. 87.
   Morris, p. 119.
   Owens (1950), p. 281.
   Raim & Dunson, p. 68.
   Randolph III, IV, p. 194.
   Sandburg, p. 316.
   Scarborough (1937), p. 364.

B. Jackson, George Pullen. *Spiritual Folk-Songs of Early America.* 1937. Reprint. New York: Dover Publications, Inc., 1964, p. 48.

Perrow, E. C. "Songs and Rhymes from the South," *Journal of American Folklore* (1915), 28: 129–190, 170.

C. Fiddlin' John Carson   Okeh 7006
   Delmore Brothers   Montgomery
                                                           Ward MW
                                                           4458
   Buell Kazee   Brunswick BR 211
                                                           Supertone 2045
   Ernest Stoneman   Edison 52077

D. Delmore Brothers   *In Memory of the Delmore Brothers, Vol. II.* King 920.
   Buell Kazee   *Mountain Banjo Songs and Tunes.* County 515.
   Otis Pierce   *Every Bush and Tree.* Bay 102.
   Almeda Riddle   *Granny Riddle's Songs and Ballads.* Minstrel JD-203.
   —   *Songs and Ballads of the Ozarks.* Vanguard VRS 9158.
   The Virginia Drifters   *A Delmore Brothers Tribute.* Old Homestead OHS 80007.
   Doc Watson   *Old Time Music at Newport.* Vanguard VRS 9147.
   —   *Old Timey Concert.* Vanguard VSD 107/8.

Indexes

Index of Titles

Index of First Lines

Index of Locations

Index of Informants

About the Editor

A native of North Carolina, W. K. McNeil is the folklorist at the Ozark Folk Center in Mountain View, Arkansas. He earned an M.A. from the Cooperstown Graduate Program at the State University of New York, and a Ph.D. in Folklore from Indiana University. Author of many studies on American folklore and editor of two other anthologies, *The Charm is Broken* and *Ghost Stories from the American South,* McNeil is also the general editor of the American Folklore Series.